Lessons on
the Holy Spirit

LESSONS
ON THE
Holy
Spirit

George Davis King

BROADMAN PRESS
Nashville, Tennessee

Dewey Decimal Classification: 231.3
Subject Heading: HOLY SPIRIT
Library of Congress Catalog Card Number: 87-26804
Printed in the United States of America

Library of Congress Cataloging-in-Publication Data

King, George Davis, 1950-
    Lessons on the Holy Spirit.

    Bibliography: p.
    1. Holy Spirit.   2. Gifts, Spiritual.   I. Title.
BT121.2.K52   1988   231'.3   87-26804
ISBN 0-8054-1153-4

Dedication

To
my wife Alene
and
our daughter April

Acknowledgments

In a sense this book is the work of many authors, combined under one cover on one single subject. It was done as a personal learning experience concerning the ministry of the Holy Spirit. I acknowledge considerable benefit from the books and teachings I have gained over the past few years.

Sifting through mountains of materials on the subject of the Holy Spirit, I experienced this need to know more about the Spirit's personal work in my life. With this purpose in mind I make it available to you so it may cause you to grow deeper in Christ and experience more of the controlling influence of the Holy Spirit in your life. I have received more from the thoughts of others than I am able to give.

I am deeply appreciative to my wife, Alene, and daughter, April, for supporting me with the many hours of prayer and patience they have experienced in my writing this study manual. Truly, they have given constant evidence of being controlled by the Spirit.

Lessons 2, 6, 12, 13, 14, and 15 are a free adaptation of Campus Crusade for Christ's study manual, *Ten Basic Steps Toward Christian Maturity: Step 3, The Christian and the Holy Spirit*. The material and the one illustration are used by permission.

This study manual should be helpful to faithful believers who desire a deeper study of the Holy Spirit, as well as to ministers and others who are called to make presentations to their congregations and other hearers. I humbly pray this book will edify and enrich its readers.

George Davis King, Jr.

Contents

LESSON 1

The Displaced Member of the Trinity

Did you receive the Holy Spirit when you believed? And they said unto him, "No, we have not even heard whether there be a Holy Spirit" (Acts 19:2).

Even the Spirit of truth whom the world cannot receive because it does not behold Him or know Him, but YOU KNOW HIM, because He abides with you and will be in you (John 14:17).

AIM: To show there there is a personality of the Trinity, God the Holy Spirit, who exists as an unseen reality in the believer's life

INTRODUCTION: A. W. Tozer wrote: "In most Christian churches, the Spirit is entirely overlooked. Whether He is present or absent makes no real difference to anyone. Brief reference is made to Him in the Doxology and the Benediction. Further than that, He might as well not exist. So completely do we ignore Him that it is only courtesy that we can be called Trinitarian . . . The idea of the Spirit held by the average Church member is so vague as to be nearly non-existent."

If this statement were only half true, it should challenge us to deal with this ignorance that paralyzes the effectiveness and ministry of churches. Through this series on the Holy Spirit, we will discover some facts concerning Him and His ministry in our lives. Such topics range from Why the Holy Spirit was sent, sins against the Spirit, the fruit of the Spirit, the gifts of the Spirit, and the deity and personality of The Spirit.

LESSON:

I. DO YOU KNOW THE HOLY SPIRIT?

"A preacher was about to deliver a carefully prepared message when there came to him the conviction that it was not appropriate to the group of people before him. He reluctantly abandoned his manuscript, and seeking the Spirit's guidance, decided to read John 14.

"As he read, he was alert to discern the message for the occasion. Nor was he disappointed. On reaching verse 7, three words gripped his attention—'Ye know Him'—God the Father. He read two more verses and a second clause became apparent—'Hast thou known Me?'—God the Son. When he reached verse 17, a third sentence stopped him—'But ye know Him'—God the Holy Spirit.

"These words struck home with tremendous force. Did he really know Him? 'I know God the Father,' he considered to himself, 'and I have experienced much of His paternal love and care. I know God the Son, for is He not my Savior and Lord with whom I daily commune? But I cannot say that I know the Holy Spirit in any comparable and personal way.'"[1]

The question: Do you know the Holy Spirit in a personal way? How can you get to know Him?

II. WE CAN KNOW *HIM* BY *EXPERIENCE*

"In our Scripture, Acts 19:2, Paul asked the twelve disciples of John, 'Did you receive the Holy Spirit when you believed?' Their response was, 'No, we have not even heard whether there be a Holy Spirit.' Not many of us would return such an answer today for we are familiar with the Covenant and Doxologies of our faith. But to some believers, the Spirit is still 'it' rather than 'He.' They know there is a Holy Spirit but conceive of Him as an intangible power or influence—but not as a real divine Person who can be known and loved and worshiped. Some believers are strict in their doctrine (teachings) and know a great deal about the Spirit, but do not know Him in the sense implied above. The word 'know' means knowledge which is gained by experience, not just intellectual apprehension of facts. It is one thing to know Him personally. The difference is like that between knowing all about food, even possessing it, and eating and enjoying it. One is intellectual apprehension, the other is knowledge gained by experience. It is not knowing about God that brings eternal life, but knowing God (John 17:3)."[2]

What do you know about the Holy Spirit? or better still, what does the Holy Spirit mean to you personally? _____

_____

_____

_____

LESSON 2

Who Is the Holy Spirit, and Why Did He Come?   Part I

But when He, the Spirit of truth, comes, He will guide you into all the truth; for He will not speak on His own initiative, but whatever He hears, He will speak; and He will disclose to you what is to come. He shall glorify Me; for He shall take of Mine, and shall disclose it to you (John 16:13-14).

AIM: To gain an understanding of the ministry of the Holy Spirit and learn how to appropriate His power for holy living and Christian service

INTRODUCTION: The majority of Christians know very little about the Holy Spirit. All of us have heard sermons on God the Father, and many on God the Son, but a sermon on God the Holy Spirit is rare. The Holy Spirit is equal in every way with God the Father and God the Son. He vitally affects our lives as Christians. In fact, His presence or absence in a person's life makes the difference between life and death spiritually. We are born spiritually through the ministry of the Holy Spirit, according to John 3:1-8.

LESSON:

I. THE IDENTITY OF THE HOLY SPIRIT

The Holy Spirit is known as the third Person of the Trinity: Father, Son, and Holy Spirit. He is not some vague shadow or an impersonal force. He is a Person. All of the divine attributes are ascribed to the Holy Spirit. Personality is composed of intellect (mind), emotions, and will. He has all three.

A. What in 1 Corinthians 2:1 suggests that the Holy Spirit has intellect? _____

_____

B. What in Romans 15:30 suggests that He has emotion?

_____

_____

C. Does the Holy Spirit have a will (1 Cor. 12:11)? _____

_____

_____

II. THE MINISTRY OF THE HOLY SPIRIT

Dr. J. Edwin Orr describes the Holy Spirit as: "The Commander-in-chief of the Army of Christ. He is the Lord of the Harvest, Supreme in revival, evangelism, and missionary endeavors. Without His consent, other plans are bound to fail. It behooves us as Christians to fit our tactical operations into the plan of His strategy, which is the reviving of the Church and the evangelization of the world."

The first reference to the Holy Spirit is made in Genesis 1:2. His influence is noted throughout the Old Testament but becomes more profound in the life and ministry of our Lord. Finally, after our Savior ascended to be at the right hand of the Father, the place of power, He sent the Holy Spirit to be the "Comforter" (John 14:26 and 15:26). The Greek word for Comforter is *parakletos,* meaning the "one called alongside" the Christian as a companion and friend, also the One who "energizes," "strengthens" and "empowers" the believer in Christ.

A. What was the work of the Holy Spirit in the Old Testament?

1. Job 26:13; Ps. 104:30; Gen. 1:2-3? _____

_____

_____

2. 2 Pet. 1:21; 2 Tim. 3:16? _____

_____

_____

3. 1 Sam. 16:13; 2 Chron. 15:1-2; Judges 14:5-7; 15:9-14? _____

_____

_____

B. What was the work of the Holy Spirit in Jesus' ministry?
   1. Matt. 1:18-20; Luke 1:30-35? _____

   _____

   2. John 1:32? _____
   3. Matt. 12:28? _____
   4. John 3:5-6? _____
   5. 1 Pet. 3:18; Rom. 8:11? _____

   _____

C. What do we learn about the nature and operation of the Holy Spirit in each of the following references?
   1. John 14:26 _____
   2. 1 Cor. 3:16 _____
   3. Rom. 8:2 _____
   4. 2 Cor. 4:13 _____
   5. John 16:13 _____
   6. Heb. 10:29 _____
   7. Rom. 1:4 _____
   8. 2 Tim. 1:7 _____

III. WHY DID THE HOLY SPIRIT COME?

A. What is the chief reason the Holy Spirit came? (John 16:14). _____

   _____

B. What then will be a logical result of the Holy Spirit controlling our lives? _____

   _____

C. According to John 15:8, "Herein is my Father _____
that ye _____;
so shall ye be my disciples."

IV. SUMMARY

People often give the impression that God is an impersonal force which they exploit for a life of well-being. This is wrong! God is a Person, and through His Spirit He wants to motivate and use us for His glory and our own good. We do not use God—God uses us. Through His Spirit in us He wants to call attention to Jesus Christ, the Savior, "The Way."

LESSON 3

Who Is the Holy Spirit,
and Why Did He Come?   Part II

But when He, the Spirit of truth, comes, He will guide you into all the truth; for He will not speak on His own initiative, but whatever He hears, He will speak; and He will disclose to you what is to come. He shall glorify Me; for He shall take of Mine, and shall disclose it to you (John 16:13-14).

AIM: To gain an understanding of the ministry of the Holy Spirit and learn characteristics of His personality

INTRODUCTION: The Bible teaches that the Holy Spirit is a person with characteristics of a person. He is a member of the Trinity as discussed in the previous lesson. It is essential that we as believers learn as much about the Holy Spirit's Divine Personality as we can. It will help us to be prepared for the blessing He wants to bring into our lives.

As we discussed in the last lesson, the Holy Spirit has such marks of personality as knowledge, feeling, emotion, and will. The Spirit is a real personality just as the Father and Son are personalities. This is additional information concerning His personality.

LESSON:

I. THE SPIRIT HAS KNOWLEDGE

A person must have the ability to retain knowledge in order to be a living personality. According to 1 Corinthians 2:10,11

_____

_____

the Spirit has an unlimited capacity to know all things. It is through Him that we get to hear and know God's truth. He knows all truth and reveals it in connection with the Scriptures. With this, He enlightens our minds so we can understand it.

II. HE HAS A WILL

Not only does He have knowledge, He also has a will. According to 1 Corinthians 12:11 _____

_____

we see He has a will and desires to use it in relation to our doing His will. In this list of gifts that He distributes, we see that He does so at His own pleasure. We must always keep this in mind.

III. HE HAS A MIND

Rom. 8:27 _____

_____

This means that as He dwells in us, God knows His mind and He has the capability of planning that which can operate only through a mind.

IV. HE HAS LOVE

Rom. 15:30 _____

_____

From this Scripture we learn that He has the capacity to love. In John 3:16, we see that God the Father loves us. In Philippians 2:5-8, we find that Jesus also gave evidence of His love for us. The same is true with the Spirit, for He seeks us out while we are in sin, and draws us finally to Christ. It does not stop there, for He changes us into the image of Jesus.

V. HE CAN BE GRIEVED

Eph. 4:30 _____

From this we gather that the Spirit has emotions and that He can be hurt. Only a person can express emotions, will, and an intellect. He knows our thoughts and words and is hurt if any of them are wrong.

VI. HE SEARCHES OUT THE TRUTH OF GOD
1 Cor. 2:10 _____

"The Holy Spirit searches and this searching is in realms that we cannot by ourselves enter into. The Holy Spirit not only illumines our hearts so that we can understand truth, but He Himself has first searched out the truth that He reveals to us.

VII. HE INFLUENCES US TO PRAY AND PRAYS WITHIN US
"Every believer has two Persons of the Godhead praying for him. The Lord Jesus Christ intercedes in the presence of God for us. Since he has gone through all the experiences that we have, except that of sinning, He is able to help us in our difficulties." We are exhorted in Hebrews 4:15 to _____
_____.

Also in Hebrews 7:25 _____
_____.

VIII. HE TESTIFIES
"Before He left this earth, the Lord Jesus promised in John 15:26-27 _____

The Holy Spirit testifies to us concerning the Father and Christ, and then gives us the power to testify to others of the deep truths of our faith.

IX. HE IS A TEACHER
"He not only influences us to seek God's way, but He takes us

by the hand, leads us into all truth, and teaches us the things we ought to know. Concerning this, our Lord said in John 14:26

_____

_____

_____

Only a person could have the ability to teach. This would be impossible to something nothing more than a mere influence.

X. HE HAS THE POWER AND AUTHORITY TO COMMAND AND DIRECT

"It is important that we recognize this truth. According to Acts 16:6,7, Paul wanted to go into the province of Asia to preach, but he and Timothy were forbidden by the Holy Spirit. When they came to Mysia, they attempted to go into Bithynia, but the Holy Spirit did not allow them to do so. The Holy Spirit directs and commands His servants in their ministry of the gospel. Only as this work is done under His divine leadership is it done right.

XI. HE CALLS AND APPOINTS INDIVIDUALS TO ENTER INTO THE GOSPEL MINISTRY, AND INTO THE SPECIFIC PHASES OF THE MINISTRY HE DESIGNATES

"In the church at Antioch, God's servants 'ministered to the Lord, and fasted, the Holy Ghost said, Separate me Barnabas and Saul for the work whereunto I have called them' (Acts 13:2). In reality every believer has the command of God to have a part in the work of the ministry, but it is the Spirit of God who personally appoints individuals for each specific phase of service.

XII. HE BAPTIZES ALL BELIEVERS INTO THE BODY OF CHRIST

"This is not to be confused with water baptism which is an ordinance in the local church. The baptismal work of the Holy

Spirit is in a realm that is outside our consciousness and understanding but it is real just the same. First Corinthians 12:12-13
says _____

_____

According to this passage each individual believer is made a vital
part of the Church, the Body of Christ, through this operation
of the Spirit. This might be illustrated from the human body
whose different members grow cell by cell in the human em-
bryo. The Spirit of God baptizes us or places us into the mystical
body of the Lord Jesus Christ.

XIII. HE IMPARTS GIFTS FOR SERVICE

1 Cor. 12:8-11 _____

_____

_____

Rom. 12:3-8 _____

_____

_____

Eph. 4:7-11 _____

_____

_____

"From these and related passages we can safely conclude
that no believer is without some gift from the Spirit for service.
These are given at the will and discretion of the Holy Spirit who
'divides to every man severally as he will' (1 Cor. 12:11). Believers do not choose these gifts for themselves. The Spirit of
God makes these decisions and choices because He is a Person
and, therefore, can plan and think and organize.

XIV. HE GUIDES AND ENERGIZES IN ALL SERVICE FOR CHRIST

The testimony of Zechariah 4:6 is _____

_____

"The Spirit of God endues the believer with power for whatever service he has been chosen to do. The Lord's work done in human wisdom and human strength is useless; but done in the power and energy of His Spirit, it is eternal in its quality and blessing.

XV. SUMMARY

"In speaking of the Holy Spirit being a person we must recognize that His personality is not a human personality but a personality of a deity. These personality traits though similar to ours are on the divine level, whereas ours are on the human level."[1]

LESSON 4

Who Is the Holy Spirit, and Why Did He Come?   Part III

But when He, the Spirit of truth, comes, He will guide you into all the truth; for He will not speak on His own initiative, but whatever He hears, He will speak; and He will disclose to you what is to come. He shall glorify Me; for He shall take of Mine, and shall disclose it to you (John 16:13-14).

AIM: To gain an understanding of the ministry of the Holy Spirit and learn some of His attributes as God

INTRODUCTION: Throughout the Bible, it is clear that the Holy Spirit is God Himself. This is seen in the attributes which are given to the Holy Spirit in Scripture. Without exception these attributes are those of God Himself.

LESSON:

I. "HE IS ETERNAL

Heb. 9:14 _____

_____

This means that there never was a time when He was not. Only God is from everlasting to everlasting. Man has a temporal existence and those who trust in Christ have eternal life, but man has a beginning. God has no beginning. So when the Scriptures speak of the ETERNAL SPIRIT they are describing One who is a member of the Trinity.

II. "HE IS ALL-POWERFUL (THAT IS, OMNIPOTENT)

Luke 1:35 _____

_____

Here the Holy Spirit is described as "the power of the Highest." He has power for anything and for everything that He needs to do. This is an attribute belonging to God only.

III. "HE IS EVERYWHERE PRESENT (THAT IS, OMNIPRESENT) AT THE SAME TIME

Ps. 139:7-10 _____

_____

The Holy Spirit is not limited to one place at one time. He is present everywhere all the time and at all times. This proves that He is God.

IV. "HE IS ALL-KNOWING (THAT IS, OMNISCIENT)

1 Cor. 2:10-11 _____

_____

_____

He knows all things. Nothing is unknown to Him from eternity to eternity. You and I know part and see things as in a mirror darkly, but nothing is hidden from the Spirit of God.

V. "HE IS CALLED GOD

Acts 5:3-4 _____

_____

_____

2 Cor. 3:18 _____

_____

_____

VI. "HE IS THE CREATOR

The first biblical reference to the Holy Spirit is Genesis 1:1.

_____

_____

The word *Elohim* translated 'God' in this verse is a name in the Hebrew language which shows a plural unity—more than two—thus is a veiled reference to the Triune God. It was the Triune God who created the heaven and the earth. In Genesis 1:2, we learn _____

_____.

Only God could bring into being something that did not previously exist. To create means to make something where nothing existed before. Where the word 'create' is used in this sense, only God could be the subject. No one else can create. The Holy Spirit as God was active in the work of creation.

VII. "HE GIVES SPIRITUAL LIFE

John 3:3 _____

_____

John 3:5 _____

_____

The creating and giving of life is possible only with the eternal God. The impartation of spiritual life is attributed to the Holy Spirit which proves that He is a member of the Godhead.

VIII. "HE IS THE AUTHOR OF THE WORD

2 Pet. 1:21 _____

_____

The Bible is not a book that men would write if they could. It is the kind of book, however, that they could not write. Its words are the words of the eternal God; its Divine Author is the Spirit of God. This is another proof that He is God.

IX. SUMMARY

"There is nothing that God is that the Holy Spirit is not. All of the essential aspects of Deity belong to the Holy Spirit. We can say of Him exactly what was said of Jesus Christ in the ancient Nicene Creed: He is very God of very God! So we bow before Him, we worship Him, we accord Him every response Scripture requires of our relationship to almighty God.

"WHO IS THE HOLY SPIRIT. HE IS GOD!!!!!!!!"[1]

LESSON 5

Who Is the Holy Spirit, and Why Did He Come?　Part IV

But when He, the Spirit of truth, comes, He will guide you into all the truth; for He will not speak on His own initiative, but whatever He hears, He will speak; and He will disclose to you what is to come. He shall glorify Me; for He shall take of Mine, and shall disclose it to you (John 16:13-14).

AIM: To give a review of previous lessons and to give additional insight into the Deity of the Holy Spirit according to the Scriptures

INTRODUCTION: As we have discussed earlier, the Holy Spirit is God and is equal to both the Father and the Son. We should never speak of Him as "It" or consider Him only an influence. He is distinctly God the Holy Spirit and separate from the other two persons of the Godhead. In Genesis, he was active in creation, and in the Old Testament, He temporarily empowered persons for service and departed when disobedience occurred.

For example, when David sinned, he prayed Psalm 51:11

_____

_____

When Pentecost occurred, the Spirit began to indwell believers permanently, giving him/her power for service. Let us review some aspects of the Deity of the Holy Spirit.

LESSON:

I. REVIEW

Acts 5:3,4 _____

_____

_____

   In this occurrence, Peter revealed the Deity of the Spirit when he told Ananias and Sapphira that they had lied not to men but to God. Calling Him God means that He is co-equal with the Father and the Son.

II. THE DEITY OF THE SPIRIT IS SUGGESTED IN HIS DIVINE ATTRIBUTES

1. According to Psalm 139:7-10, He is present everywhere at the same time.
2. According to Luke 1:35, He has all power.
3. According to 1 Corinthians 2:10,11, He also has all knowledge.
4. According to Hebrews 9:14, He is eternal.

III. HE IS EQUAL TO THE FATHER AND SON

His equality is evident in two instances.

1. In the baptism of believers (Matt. 28:19 _____
   _____).
2. In a benediction (2 Cor. 13:14 _____
   _____).

IV. HE WAS PRESENT IN THE MINISTRY AND LIFE OF CHRIST

Luke 1:35 _____

_____

He was conceived by the Spirit.
Acts 10:38 _____

_____

He was appointed by the Spirit for service.
Matt. 4:1 _____

_____

He was led by the Spirit.
Heb. 9:14 _____

_____

He was crucified in the power of the Spirit.
Rom. 8:11 _____

_____

He was even raised from the dead by the power of the Spirit.
Acts 1:2 _____

_____

He gave commandments to his disciples through the Spirit.

V. SUMMARY

If Christ.was dependent upon the Spirit during His sojourn
here on planet earth, what about our dependency?

LESSON 6

How Is the Holy Spirit Related to Every Christian? Part I

And do not get drunk with wine, for this is dissipation, but be filled with the Spirit (Eph. 5:18).

AIM: To show how the Holy Spirit is related to every believer

INTRODUCTION: A Christian is one who has received Jesus Christ into his/her life as Lord and Savior according to John 1:12, John 3:5, and 2 Corinthians 5:17.

LESSON:

I. THINGS THAT TAKE PLACE AT CONVERSION

At the time of the new birth, several things happen to believers.

1. John 3:5 _____
2. 1 Cor. 3:16 _____
3. Eph. 4:30 _____
4. 1 Cor. 12:13 _____
5. 2 Cor. 5:5 _____

At the moment of spiritual birth every Christian is regenerated, indwelt, sealed, guaranteed, baptized, and filled with the Holy Spirit. The act of regenerating, indwelling, sealing, guaranteeing, and baptizing the Christian into the body of Christ by the Holy Spirit is a positional relationship and may or may not be accompanied by an especially emotional experience.

6. The Holy Spirit fills *every yielded* Christian for service. Every Christian must be filled with the Holy Spirit for power to be a more effective witness for Christ. Acts 1:8 says

_____

_____

_____.

Every Biblical reference to filling with the Holy Spirit, both in the Old Testament and in the New Testament, is related to power for service and witness.

II. WHAT DOES THE SPIRIT DO FOR EVERY BELIEVER?

Summarize in your own words what the Holy Spirit does for the Christian according to:

1. Rom. 8:16 _____

_____

2. Rom. 8:26-27 _____

_____

III. THE REASON WE ARE FILLED WITH THE SPIRIT

What is the main reason we are to be filled with the Spirit? (Acts 1:8, 4:29,31). _____

_____

_____

IV. A COMMANDMENT TO FOLLOW

According to Ephesians 5:18, is it commanded or suggested that we be filled with the Spirit? _____

V. THREE ADDITIONAL RESULTS OF BEING FILLED

What are three additional results of being filled with the Spirit? (Eph. 5:19-21). _____

_____

_____

VI. CAN A CHRISTIAN NOT HAVE THE HOLY SPIRIT?

Can a person be a Christian and not have the Holy Spirit in him/her? (Rom. 8:9). _____

_____

VII. WHAT DOES IT TAKE TO HAVE A SUCCESSFUL LIFE?

What work of the Holy Spirit is necessary for a successful Christian life and service? (Eph. 5:18). _____

_____

_____

VIII. SUMMARY

It is evident that the Holy Spirit plays a major role in the life of a Christian. God carries out His purpose in the life of the Christian through the control of the Holy Spirit. To be a successful Christian one must yield to His control.

LESSON 7

How Is the Holy Spirit Related to Every Christian?   Part II

Regeneration

And do not get drunk with wine, for that is dissipation, but be filled with the Spirit (Eph. 5:18).

Jesus answered and said unto him, Verily, verily, I say unto thee, Except a man be born again, he cannot see the kingdom of God (John 3:3, KJV).

AIM: To show how the Holy Spirit is related to every believer by the aspect of regeneration

INTRODUCTION: At the moment of salvation, the Holy Spirit begins His work in a believer's life with regeneration. According to Ephesians 2:1, we were _____

_____.

Only through the new birth can this dead life be replaced. Only in Christ can we ever receive the new life that He alone can give, and it is only possible through the ministry of the Holy Spirit.

Regeneration is an action of God to bring new life to the person who trusts in Christ. According to John 3:6, this work is done only by the Holy Spirit. Write out John 3:6 in your own words _____

_____

_____

It is not a process but an instantaneous experience that sometimes takes a lifetime to be revealed. It is a complete work done by the Holy Spirit positionally in Christ, but because we are limited in time and space, we are *being* transformed. The context is: "I am saved, I am being saved, and I will be saved."

Scripture gives us six important points on the necessity of regeneration.

LESSON:

I. REGENERATION IS OF DIVINE ORIGIN

John 1:13 _____

_____

_____

II. REGENERATION IS ESSENTIAL TO SPIRITUAL VISION

John 3:3 _____

_____

_____

III. REGENERATION BRINGS INTO BEING A NEW CREATION

2 Cor. 5:17 _____

_____

_____

IV. REGENERATION IS NECESSARY TO SALVATION

Titus 3:5 _____

_____

_____

V. REGENERATION IS THROUGH THE WORD OF GOD

1 Pet. 1:23 _____

_____

_____

VI. REGENERATION IS OBTAINED BY FAITH

1 John 5:1 _____

_____

_____

VII. SUMMARY

The Spirit has many different relationships with believers but only the Spirit can re-create a person. He gives him a new nature, the nature of God. Look up the following Scriptures, then observe and record the different aspects of the Holy Spirit's relationship with the believer.

Titus 3:5 _____

_____

_____

John 3:3-7 _____

_____

_____

_____

_____

1 Pet. 1:23 _____

_____

_____

James 1:18 _____

_____

_____

LESSON 8

How Is the Holy Spirit Related to Every Christian? Part III

Indwelling

And do not get drunk with wine, for that is dissipation, but be filled with the Spirit (Eph. 5:18).

Even the Spirit of truth; whom the world cannot receive, because it seeth Him not, neither knoweth Him: but ye know Him; for He DWELLETH with you, and shall be IN you (John 14:17, KJV).

AIM: To show how the Holy Spirit is related to every believer by the aspect of indwelling

INTRODUCTION: The Holy Spirit indwells the believing sinner. In other words, He not only joins us to the Savior (through spiritual baptism, to be discussed in a later lesson), but He joins Himself to us. Jesus, prior to His crucifixion, predicted both of these ministries.

There is no clearer truth in the Scriptures than this: that all believers are indwelt by the Holy Spirit. In 1 Corinthians 3:16,17, Paul wrote _____

_____

In chapter 6:19, he wrote _____

_____.

From this short observation we find that the principle of the Spirit's indwelling has scriptural foundation.

LESSON:

I. WHAT IS THE PURPOSE OF THE INDWELLING MINISTRY OF THE HOLY SPIRIT?

Look up the following verses and record your answer.

2 Cor. 5:17 _____

_____

_____

Gal. 5:16-18 _____

_____

_____

Eph. 3:16 _____

_____

_____

II. IS THERE A DIFFERENCE BETWEEN INDWELLING AND FILLING (OR CONTROLLING) BY THE HOLY SPIRIT?

"The indwelling of the Holy Spirit does not depend upon our consciousness of that indwelling. Whether we feel we are indwelt or feel we are not indwelt has nothing to do with it. We are the temple of God and the Spirit of God dwells in us, according to 1 Corinthians 3:16. This is not qualified by whether or not we feel like it. This is a truth for every believer. Since God says this is so, it is. Note: Even the carnal Christian is indwelt by the Spirit of God. Though carnal, he is still a believer."[1]

III. WHAT IS THE BASIS FOR THE INDWELLING OF THE HOLY SPIRIT?

"Faith in Christ as our Savior is our basis for the indwelling Spirit, not our behavior. The filling/controlling of the Holy Spirit has to do with our behavior, but His indwelling has to do with our first act of faith when we trusted in Christ. His indwelling is a permanent matter. It is a once for all thing."[2]

IV. SUMMARY

"Sin does not expel the Holy Spirit from our lives but without fail it will bring conviction to our hearts. For the Holy Spirit to remove Himself when a Christian sins would be to leave that Christian without conviction and without life. If such were possible, it would mean He would be unborn and the new birth would have to be repeated over and over again.

"Every time we sin, it is the filling/controlling of the Holy Spirit and the power that is affected by sin, not the indwelling. *The evidence for the indwelling Spirit is not our experience but the Word of God.* He declares it and that should settle it. We are not to look for fruit as the evidence of the indwelling but we are to believe God. He cannot lie. He would not deceive us. The fruit of the Spirit, on the other hand, will be witnessed when we are controlled by the Holy Spirit."[3]

LESSON 9

How Is the Holy Spirit Related to Every Christian?   Part IV

Sealing

And do not get drunk with wine, for this is dissipation, but be filled with the Spirit (Eph. 5:18).

Who also SEALED us and gave us the Spirit in our hearts as a pledge (1 Cor. 1:22).

AIM: To show how the Holy Spirit is related to every believer by the aspect of sealing

INTRODUCTION: At conversion, several events occur at the same time. One of these is SEALING. Believers may not be aware of it ever happening, but it occurs nevertheless. We will define what sealing means and discuss the different types of seals.

LESSON:

I. THE SEAL

The word seal comes from the Greek word *sphragizo*, which means to authorize, validate, or guarantee. It is used three times in the New Testament in relationship to believers. Jesus was also sealed in John 6:27, where John wrote _____

_____.

In this Scripture, God the Father sealed the Son.

At the moment of salvation, believers are sealed with the Holy Spirit for the day of redemption as stated in Ephesians 1:13 _____

_____

_____.

Sealing has several contexts in which they relate to the believer and the Holy Spirit. Let's look at some.

II. THE SEAL OF SECURITY

Paul had two thoughts in mind when he suggested that we are sealed by the Holy Spirit. The first is security, and the second is ownership. We will look at security in this section.

The security of a seal is illustrated in Daniel, when the King had Daniel placed in the lion's den. Doing so, he sealed it so Daniel could not get out and no one else could get in. In Esther, a decree was made that affected all of the Jews, and it was sealed with the king's ring and no one could revoke it, not even the king himself. He had to issue another decree that countermanded the previous decree. In the New Testament, Pilate did the same thing when he ordered the soldiers to secure the tomb of Christ in Matthew 27:65,66 _____

_____

_____

The word seal in this passage is the same Greek word used in the other passages that talk of the sealing of the Holy Spirit. A. T. Robertson wrote that the sealing of the stone was "probably by a cord stretched across the stone and sealed at each end as in Daniel 6:17. The sealing was done in the presence of the Roman guards who were left in charge to protect this stamp of Roman authority and power."[1] As a result, when the Holy Spirit seals us, we are secure in Christ. Paul states in Romans 8:38-39 that _____

_____

_____.

If this is not secure enough, then nothing else will do.

III. THE SEAL OF OWNERSHIP

In this aspect of sealing, it means total ownership by one who has paid the purchase price. We have been bought with a price that Christ paid on the cross, and now He is the owner. When something is bought, usually a mark is made as to who owns it. When we were bought by Christ, He placed His own mark on us and it was the Holy Spirit. He is a pledge of the inheritance that we will receive one day. The Spirit is God's pledge, a down payment, of all that He has promised us, and it is a very good down payment!

The New Testament refers to this down payment three times. Look up the following references and record your insights as to the type of down payment that the Holy Spirit makes to us.

2 Cor. 1:22 _____

_____

Here the Spirit's presence in our lives is God's pledge that He will fulfill His promise.

2 Cor. 5:5 _____

_____

The context here suggests that the Spirit in our lives is God's pledge that we shall receive spiritual bodies at Christ's coming.

Eph. 1:14 _____

_____

Here the Spirit is God's pledge guaranteeing our inheritance until the future brings the total redemption of those who are God's possession."[2]

IV. SUMMARY

When we are baptized into the Body of Christ, the Spirit enters our lives and by His presence seals us. He is God's pledge assuring us of our inheritance to come. Only God can break the seal that He Himself has established. Any seal that a man makes, God can break, but any seal God makes, only He can break. God has promised He will not break this seal, for the seal is the Holy Spirit, and His presence with us is the assurance of our security "unto the day of redemption." This sealing is only for those who have turned in faith to Christ and have been regenerated. Let us not build false hopes on human merit or any system of salvation other than salvation by grace through faith in Christ.

LESSON 10

How Is the Holy Spirit Related to Every Christian?　Part V

Baptism of The Holy Spirit

And do not get drunk with wine, for that is dissipation, but be filled with the Spirit (Eph. 5:18).

For by one Spirit we were all BAPTIZED into one body, whether Jews or Greeks, whether slaves or free; and we were all made to drink of one Spirit (1 Cor. 12:13).

AIM: To show how the Holy Spirit is related to every believer by the aspect of baptism

INTRODUCTION: According to Scripture, there is only one baptism with the Holy Spirit in the life of a believer, and it takes place at the moment of salvation. It commenced at Pentecost, and now all who come to know Christ as Lord and Savior share the same experience. They are baptized at the moment of regeneration. In addition, they may be filled (to be taught in Lessons 12—14) with the Holy Spirit. If not they need to be.

LESSON:

I. THE SCRIPTURAL USAGE OF THE WORD BAPTISM

According to the Scripture, when the word baptism was used, it is always in the context of an initiatory experience that is never repeated. In the case of water baptism, it is never stated or implied that a believer needs to be rebaptized at some point in his/her life. The same is true for baptism in the Spirit. It too is an initiatory experience of entering into the kingdom. The Bible

44

never suggests or implies that Spirit baptism should be repeated. For a scriptural foundation, look up 1 Corinthians 12:13 and write it out in your own words. _____

_____

_____

_____

From the original Greek, this verse suggests that baptism is an act that was done in the past, was completed, and need not be done again. There are two facts this verse reveals:
"1. The baptism with the Spirit is a collective operation of the Spirit of God.
2. The baptism with the Spirit includes every believer.
Dr. W. Graham Scroggie once said, 'observe carefully to whom the apostle is writing and of whom he is speaking. He uses the word "all"—It is not to the faithful Thessalonians, nor to the liberal Philippians, nor to the spiritual Ephesians, but to the carnal Corinthians (1 Cor. 3:1).' The clear indication is that baptism with the Spirit is connected with our *standing* before God, not our current subjective *state;* with our *position* and not our *experience.*"[1]

II. BAPTISM AND FILLING

There is a marked difference between baptism and filling. They are opposite in meaning. When we talk about baptism, we are suggesting that we are submerged into an element, such as water or the Spirit. When we talk about filling, we are suggesting that an element is put into us. When we are baptized, we are put into the Spirit. When we are filled, the Spirit is in us. The baptism of the Spirit is an initial act at conversion and is never repeated. The filling can be repeated any number of times, for filling means controlling and sometimes the Holy Spirit is not in control of our lives.

As it relates to baptism, it is an historical event. The filling on the other hand is a human experience that is continual.

III. BAPTIZED INTO THE BODY OF CHRIST

Write out 1 Corinthians 12:13 below. _____

_____

_____

"Four facts emerge from this text:
1. This baptism is *common to all* believers, and not the experience of a select few. The tense is *'we were all baptized'* (NASB). This 'all' included some who had even been guilty of immorality and eating food sacrificed to idols.
2. It is *a past event* in the believer's life.
3. It refers to the believer being *incorporated* into the Body of Christ by a vital, organic union effected by the Holy Spirit. Through this union he is 'in Christ' with all the resultant benefits and blessings.
4. There is *no distinction among believers* in this respect. The baptism assures the unity of the members who constitute the body."[2]

IV. SUMMARY

The Holy Spirit has been active in every age, but His baptismal work is limited to the church age. For only in this age are people made members of the body of Christ. Being baptized is not limited to some believers, but it is for all who accept Christ as Lord and Savior.

All believers are baptized by the Spirit at the moment of conversion and only at that time. It is never repeated. In writing to the Corinthians, Paul wrote to both carnal and spiritual believers and stated in 1 Corinthians 12:13, that all were baptized into the body of Christ. In Ephesians 4:5, he also stated that there is only one faith, one Lord, and one baptism. He declared in Ephesians 5:18 that we are commanded to be filled with the Spirit. Nowhere is there a command to be baptized in the Spirit. We are exhorted to be filled with the Spirit but not to be baptized.

LESSON 11

How Is the Holy Spirit Related to Every Christian?   Part VI

The Fullness of The Spirit

And do not get drunk with wine, for that is dissipation, but be filled with the Spirit (Eph. 5:18).

AIM: To show how the Holy Spirit is related to every believer by the aspect of filling with the Holy Spirit

INTRODUCTION: According to Ephesians 5:18, the Christian should be filled with the Spirit. This aspect of the work of the Holy Spirit is experiential, that is, it has to do with our daily experiences, our daily walk as Christians. The FILLING of the Holy Spirit has to do with the activity of the newfound spiritual life within us. This is not the release of new physical energy but the release of spiritual power that operates within us with the Holy Spirit as the Source. The FILLING of the Spirit is essential for spiritual growth. Without this aspect of the Spirit's work, we could not go on to maturity in the Christian life.

LESSON:

I. DEFINITION

Ephesians 5:18 states that _____
_____.

From this command, we gather that being filled is comparable to being drunk. It is being under the controlling influence of and by an agent that is not a part of the body. The alcoholic is dominated by an intoxicant that causes changes in his behavior, his thinking, and his emotions. Not only does he know about the changes that occur, others around him know it as well.

This is the idea of being filled. The Bible teaches that believers are constantly full of something, either of self's influence or full of the Spirit's influence. When we are full of self we do not fully have the Spirit's influence operating in our lives. Galatians 5:16 states _____

_____.

If we walk in the Spirit, the influence of self will become less and less. The question is not whether or not we are controlled, but by whom are we controlled. The command to be filled is again found in Ephesians 5:18b _____

_____.

The key to interpreting this verse is the verb. In the original Greek, the verb is a present passive imperative that suggests an action which has begun in the past and is continued into the future. The Greek word is *pleroō,* which means to be filled. In the imperative tense as this verb is, it means *you* be filled, a command and not a suggestion. The root idea of the word is to control. It should be an habitual action—to be filled.

In no way does this word suggest a quantitative amount of a substance that we can possess at will. When you have the Spirit, you have *all* of Him. A clear understanding of this principle is how much control does the Spirit have over you? If He has little control, He has none. It is all or none. There is no partial control.

II. THE LAW OF COMMAND AND SUPPLY

Someone once stated: "What He commands, He supplies; What He denies, He fulfills!" God, giving us a command to act upon in Ephesians 5:18, does not give us the order without providing the resources to do it. His responsibility is to help us. Ephesians 3:20, _____

_____,

suggests that in relation to doing His will, He will give us what we need, and it could well be beyond what we even ask or think.

What is the purpose of being filled? Is it for our own benefit or for His will? The answer is that He will fill us to enable us to *be* what He has called us to *be* and to *do* what He has called us to *do*. Ephesians 2:10 suggests His purpose in our lives. What is it? _____

_____

III. THE TEST OF BEING FILLED

Being in Christ, how can I know if I am under the total influence of the Spirit or under some other influence? The test is simple. When we are under the influence of the Spirit, everything we think, do, or say will point toward Christ as the reason of the hope within us. Directing others to Christ is the test. Does your life and everything in it point to Christ? Take a short inventory right now. If the results are not favorable, spend time in prayer, confessing to Him according to 1 John 1:9.

IV. SCRIPTURAL EXAMPLES OF BEING FILLED (CONTROLLED) BY THE SPIRIT

Look up the following scriptural examples of people who were controlled by the Spirit. Determine what evidence there is as to whether or not they were indeed controlled. Record your findings below.

1. Deacons (Acts 6:3) _____

_____

2. Stephen (Acts 6:5,8-10, 7:54-60) _____

_____

_____

_____

3. Peter (Acts 4:8,31) _____

_____

4. Philip (Acts 6:5, 8:5-13,35-40) _____

_____

_____

_____

Just as the influence of the Spirit can do good, it can also be abused. Look up Acts 8:9-23 and observe Simon the sorcerer and how he abused the truth of the Spirit. Record your observations below.

_____

_____

_____

_____

V. SUMMARY

As we have discussed earlier, the test of knowing whether I am full of the Spirit is whether my life continually points to Christ. Pray concerning specific areas in your life that you feel need more work on by the Spirit, points where you need to decrease control and where He needs to increase His control. Ask for His help in these areas, and ask others to join with you in this prayer so they may observe the changes taking place in your life. 1 Tim. 4:15 _____

_____

_____

LESSON 12

How Can a Christian Be Filled with the Holy Spirit?

And do not get drunk with wine for that is dissipation, but be filled with the Spirit (Eph. 5:18).

AIM: To discuss how a believer is filled with the Holy Spirit

INTRODUCTION: First, just as there are many different emotional responses to receiving Jesus Christ as Lord and Savior, so are there different experiences of being filled with the Holy Spirit. For example, one person responds to the invitation to receive Christ in an evangelistic campaign, another kneels quietly in the privacy of his home and accepts Christ. Both are born-again, and their lives are changed by the power of Christ. Of course, there are scores of other circumstances and experiences through which sincere persons meet the Savior and become "new creatures" in Christ.

In like manner, and in different ways, sincere Christians are filled with the Spirit. It should be made clear at this point that to be "filled with the Spirit" does not mean that we receive *more* of the Holy Spirit, *but that we give Him more of ourselves*. As we yield our lives to the Holy Spirit and are filled with His presence, He has greater freedom to work in and through our lives in order to exalt and glorify Christ better.

God is too great to be placed in a man-made mold. However, there are certain spiritual laws that are unchangeable. Since the Holy Spirit already dwells within every Christian, it is no longer necessary to "wait in Jerusalem" as Jesus instructed the disciples to do, except to make personal preparation for His empowering. The Holy Spirit will fill us with His power the moment we are fully yielded. It is possible for a person to be at a quiet retreat and become filled with the Holy Spirit. It is likewise possible for one to be filled with the Holy Spirit while walking down a busy street in a large city. It is even possible for one to be filled with the Holy Spirit and know something wonderful has happened, yet be completely ignorant at the time of what has actually taken place, provided one has a genuine desire to yield his will to the Lord Jesus Christ.

LESSON:

I. YOUR LOVE FOR CHRIST

A desire to serve Him and help others find Him should be your motive for being filled with the Holy Spirit.

II. WE ARE COMMANDED TO BE FILLED WITH THE SPIRIT

A. What is the admonition found in Ephesians 5:18? _____

_____

This is an admonition of God. Do you think He would ask you to do something beyond which you are able to experience? _____

III. WE SHALL RECEIVE POWER FOR WITNESSING WHEN WE ARE FILLED

A. Why do we need to be filled with the Spirit?
1. Gal. 5:22,23 _____

_____

_____

2. Acts 1:8 _____

_____

The fruit of the Spirit is never an end in itself, but only a means to the end that we win men and women to Christ, which in turn will bring glory and honor to Him. John 15:8

_____

_____

_____

If you have no desire to be Christ's witness or if you have no power in your witness, you may be sure you are not filled with the Holy Spirit. The Holy Spirit came in order for the disciples, and for you and for me, to receive power. Why do we need power? To be Christ's witnesses right where we are and to the remotest parts of the earth. Can you sincerely testify that this is your motive for wanting to be filled with the Holy Spirit? _____

IV. "IF ANY MAN IS THIRSTY, LET HIM COME TO ME AND DRINK"

A. What is a prerequisite to being filled with the Spirit (according to John 7:37)? _____

_____

and Matthew 5:6 _____

_____.

When a Christian is ready to respond to the gracious invitation of our blessed Savior, "If any man is thirsty, let him come to Me and drink," he is prepared to relinquish his will for the will of God. Therefore, this third step involves a complete surrender of your will, without reservation, to the will of God. You have come to the place where you joyfully anticipate knowing and doing His will because you realize God is loving and trustworthy and that His will is best.

Until this moment the Holy Spirit has just been a "guest" in your life, for He came to live in you the moment you became a Christian. Sometimes He was locked up in a small closet, while you used the rest of the house for your own pleasure. Now you want Him to be more than a guest—as a matter of fact, you want to turn over the title deed of your life to Him and give Him the keys to every room. You invite the Holy Spirit into the library of your mind, the dining room of your appetites, the parlor of your relationships, the game room of your social life. You invite Him into the small, hidden rooms where you have previously engaged in secret, shameful activities. All of this is past. Now, He is the Master! The challenge of Romans 12:1-2 has become clear and meaningful to you and you want to ". . . present your body a living and holy sacrifice, acceptable to God, which is your spiritual service of worship." And you no longer want to be conformed to this world, but you want to be transformed by the renewing of your mind, "that you may prove what the will of God is, that which is good and acceptable and perfect."

1. How do you know that your body is the temple of the Holy Spirit who lives within you? You are not your own anymore for you were bought with the precious blood of the Lord Jesus; therefore, you now want to glorify God in your body and in your spirit, which are God's. 1 Cor. 6:19-20 _____

_____

_____

2. Now, with all of your heart, you want to seek first the kingdom of God. Matt. 6:33 _____

_____

3. Now you want to seek "the things above, where Christ is, seated at the right hand of God. For you have died, and your life is hidden with Christ in God." Col. 3:1,3

_____

_____

4. Now you can say with "joy unspeakable," as Paul did, in Galatians 2:20 _____

_____

You have exchanged your life for the life of Christ.

5. The Spirit-filled Christian life is not an easy one, though

it is a life filled with adventure and thrills, the likes of which one cannot possibly experience any other way. Whether or not we are Christians, we are going to have problems in this life. Christians or not, we will one day die. If I am going to be a Christian, I want all that God has for me, and I want to be all that He wants me to be. If I am to suffer at all, and one day die, why not suffer and die for the highest and best, for the Lord Jesus Christ and His gospel?

V. WE APPROPRIATE THE FILLING OF THE HOLY SPIRIT BY FAITH

If our desire to be filled with the Spirit is genuinely sincere, what will we do? (Rom. 12:1-2) _____

_____

_____

This means there can be no unconfessed sin in our lives. The Holy Spirit cannot fill an unclean vessel. The Holy Spirit waits to fill you with His power. Do not resist Him any longer. Remember that, if you are a Christian, God the Father, the Son, and the Holy Spirit are already living within you. Like a miser starving to death with a fortune in boxes and jars about his cluttered room, many Christians are starving spiritually, living in defeat, failing to utilize the spiritual fortune that is their heritage in Christ.

Like our salvation, the filling of the Holy Spirit is a gift of God—we do not and cannot earn either. Both are received by the complete yielding of our wills, in faith.

VI. EXPECT TO BE FILLED

How then are we filled with the Holy Spirit? Matt. 7:7-11

_____

_____

_____

Will the Holy Spirit fill you if you ask Him? _____
How do you know? 1 John 5:14-15 _____

What must you do when you have asked Him to fill you?
Heb. 11:6 _____

Now that you have asked the Holy Spirit to fill you, *thank Him.*
God is dependable; His Word is true. If you were sincere, He
has filled you. What should be your attitude from this day forward? 1 Thess. 5:18 _____

VII. SUMMARY

Being Spirit-filled is the norm of the Christian life. It is for
every Christian. With a Spirit-filled life the Christian will experience the joy and reality of that life; he will have power to witness. The simple prerequisites are confession, cleansing, and a
complete yielding to His will by faith.

LESSON 13

How Can a Christian Know When He Is Filled?

But the fruit of the Spirit is love, joy, peace, patience, kindness, goodness, faithfulness, gentleness, self-control; against such things there is no law (Gal. 5:22-23).

AIM: To give the believer assurance of this Spirit-filled relationship and encourage him/her to continue to walk in the Spirit by faith

INTRODUCTION: Did you sincerely follow the steps outlined in lessons 10, 11, and 12? Did you ask the Holy Spirit to fill you? If you did not, Lessons 13 and 14 will not mean much to you. Go back to Lessons 10, 11, and 12, and ask God to work in your heart. If He has filled you, you will be anxious to know Lessons 13 and 14.

LESSON:

I. THE PROMISES OF THE WORD OF GOD

There are two very good ways of knowing when you are filled with the Holy Spirit.

1. What is the primary way we know if we have been filled with the Spirit? 1 John 5:14-15 _____

_____

_____

The promises of the Word of God are the primary way we can know we are filled with the Spirit.

2. The second way is by personal experience. When you asked to be filled with the Spirit, did you feel any different?

_____

_____

Do not depend upon feelings. The promises of God's Word, not our feelings, are our authority. The Christian lives by faith (trust) in the trustworthiness of God Himself and His Word. The train diagram below illustrates the relationship between FACT (God and His Word), FAITH (Our trust in God and His Word), and FEELING (the result of our faith and obedience) John 14:21 _____

_____

The train will run with or without the caboose. However, it would be futile to attempt to pull the train by the caboose. In the same way, we as Christians do not depend upon feelings or emotions, but we place our FAITH (trust) in the trustworthiness of God and the promises of His Word.

II. THE PRIORITIES OF THE SPIRIT-FILLED LIFE

A. Do you have a new and greater love for others? _____

B. Do you have a greater love for God's Word? _____

C. Are you experiencing greater boldness, liberty, and power in witnessing? _____

If you can answer "yes" to these questions, you are filled with the Spirit.

III. THE RESULTS OF THE SPIRIT-FILLED LIFE

A. What will the Holy Spirit demonstrate in and through your life as a result of His filling you? Gal. 5:22-23 _____

_____

_____

    1. What is the fruit of the Spirit? _____

_____

_____

    2. Read Acts 1:8. Do you see this power evidenced in your life? _____

    3. Apply 1 Corinthians 12:1-11 and Ephesians 4:11 to your experience. _____

_____

B. What mannerisms, language, activities, and inconsistencies in your life do you feel hinder the Holy Spirit's fruit, power, and gifts? _____

_____

_____

C. What happens as we are occupied with Christ and allow the Holy Spirit to work in us? 2 Cor. 3:18 _____

_____

_____

V. SUMMARY

The Christian is filled with the Holy Spirit by *faith*. He continues to be filled and controlled by *faith*. Evidence of a Spirit-controlled life will be a more fruitful witness for Christ. Matt. 4:19 _____

_____

John 15:8 _____

_____

The fruit of the Spirit, Gal. 5:22-23 _____

_____

_____

_____

LESSON 14

How Can a Christian Continue
to be Filled with the Holy Spriti?

He who has My commandments and keeps them, he it is who loves Me; and He who loves Me shall be loved by My Father, and I will love him, and will disclose Myself to him (John 14:21).

AIM: To help each believer reach a point of understanding which will result in the continual filling (control) of the Holy Spirit in his daily life

INTRODUCTION: We have become so used to depending on feelings instead of facts in the Christian walk, we tend to doubt God's Word and inwardly question whether He will do what His Word promises He will. Many of us have come to realize that we have been living a powerless Christian life, and we honestly asked the Holy Spirit to fill us. Now, a few days later, you may be doubting the validity of this filling because there has been no big emotional reaction or drastic change.

Remember this, what God says is *fact* and, whether your response be calm assurance, excited enthusiasm, or no definite emotional reaction at all, you can be positive that the Spirit has filled you if you've met the qualifications we discussed in Lessons 11 and 12, surrendered your will to Christ, asked in faith, and expected Him to fill you.

LESSON: HOW TO WALK IN THE SPIRIT
I. RESULTS OF THE SPIRIT-FILLED LIFE (OTHER THAN GALATIANS 5:22-23)
A. You will have the same motive for living that Jesus had John 4:34 _____

B. You will have an exuberant, abundant life flowing over into the lives of others. John 7:37-39 _____

_____

_____

C. You will have power for witnessing and aggressive spiritual warfare. Acts 1:8 _____

_____

Phil. 4:13 _____

_____

John 14:12 _____

_____

D. You will live a life of constant prayer and intercession:
   1. Because you have the inmost self of Christ in you.
   2. Only the Holy Spirit can teach you to pray. Rom. 8:26-27 _____

_____

_____

E. You will have the character of Christ, the fruit of the Spirit. It is not my trying to live like Christ but letting Him live His life in me. Gal. 2:20 _____

_____

F. Greater understanding of Scripture—1 Cor. 2:9-13

_____

_____

_____

_____

_____

II. ABIDING

Abiding is not only communion but ministry expressed in love. 1 John 3:23 _____

_____

A. God, who is love, can manifest Himself only to those who are willing to love others. John 3:16 _____

_____;

1 John 3:16 _____

_____;

1 John 3:1 _____

_____;

1 John 4:8 _____

_____;

1 John 4:19 _____

_____;

John 13:1 _____

_____;

John 15:9 _____

_____.

B. That child of God will have the fullest manifestation of the Spirit who adopts as the deliberate purpose and principle of his life: the love of Christ instead of the love of the self.
1. He ceases to grasp all and begins to give all.
2. He ceases to seek all and begins to surrender all.
3. He ceases accenting "take care of number one," and begins to accent "let every man take care of the things of others."
4. He no longer seeks the high places but the low ones.
5. He seeks to minister instead of being ministered to.
6. He no longer seeks but shuns the praise of men.
7. He no longer seeks to save his life but to lose it for others.
8. He no longer seeks to lay up, enjoy, and be at ease, but suffer, spend, and be spent for Christ Himself.
9. He seeks to love as God loves, regardless of his treatment by others. "He is kind to the unthankful and the evil." If some grievous wrong, insult or unkindness goads you from your attitude of love, justify it not, but hasten to

confess, and find forgiveness from Him who prayed for those who murdered Him, as well as for those who loved Him.

III. SUMMARY

To have a continuous day-by-day, Spirit-filled life is God's norm for the Christian and results from cleansing, uncompromising faith which believes God and claims His promises to be truth each day, moment by moment.

The Spirit-filled life is an obedient and abiding life. Begin each day by asking God to cleanse your life according to 1 John 1:9. Present your body to the Holy Spirit according to Romans 12:1-2, and ask Him to keep you filled with with His power. Ask the Holy Spirit to lead you to people who are lost. Be sensitive to His leading. Expect others to come to Christ through your witness. Do not quench the Spirit by failing to respond. Rejoice in all things, praising God even in adversity (1 Thess. 5:18, Rom. 8:28).

LESSON 15

Why Are So Few Christians Filled with the Holy Spirit?

Do not love the world, not the things in the world. If any one loves the world, the love of the Father is not in him. For all that is in the world, the lust of the flesh and the lust of the eyes and the boastful pride of life, is not from the Father, but is from the world. And the world is passing away, and also its lusts; but the one who does the will of God abides forever (1 John 2:15-17, also see Acts 5:1-11: sin against the Holy Spirit).

AIM: To discover reasons why Christians are not filled (controlled and empowered) with the Spirit

INTRODUCTION: The basic problem is that of the will. Man is a free moral agent. God would be breaking His own spiritual laws if He forced man to do His bidding. At the time of conversion, the will of man is temporarily yielded to the will of God. Romans 10:9 states _____

_____

_____

Man must be willing to "repent," which means to turn from his own way to God's way, before he can become a child of God. However, after conversion, the heart frequently loses its "first love," the radiance and glow. The joy which accompanies the spiritual birth experience is gone, and many Christians no longer walk as they should. They no longer seek to do the will of God, but for various reasons, some of which we shall discuss, have chosen to go their own way. They have chosen to work out their own plan and purpose for life. Believing themselves to be free they become susceptible to sin, and finally they cry with the apostle Paul in Romans 7:19,20,24 _____

_____

_____

_____

_____

There is no one more miserable than a believer out of fellowship with Christ.

In this spiritual condition there is very little joy in the Christian walk, not much desire to witness for Christ, practically no concern for those who are desperately in need of the forgiveness and love of our Savior.

What are the reasons then that one, who has experienced the love and forgiveness of Christ, one who has known the joy of His presence, would reject the will of God and choose to go his own way? Why would a Christian sacrifice the power and dynamic of the Spirit-filled life in order to have his own way? There are several reasons which we will discuss.

LESSON:
I. DESCRIPTION OF SELF

How does Paul describe himself in Romans 7:19,20,24?

_____

_____

_____

_____

Why are there so many unhappy Christians? Gal. 5:16,17

_____

_____

_____

II. REASONS WHY FEW BELIEVERS ARE FILLED WITH THE SPIRIT

A. Ps. 119:105 _____

His Word contains glorious truths concerning the relationship which the Christian has with the Lord Jesus Christ,
God the Father, and the Holy Spirit. This lack of information
has kept many from appropriating the fullness of the Holy
Spirit. Think of it. Every Christian is a child of God. John
1:12 _____

_____

His sins have been forgiven, and he may continue to be
cleansed from all sin (1 John 1:7 _____

_____)
as he continues in fellowship with Christ. The Father, the
Son, and the Holy Spirit actually dwell in the heart of every
Christian, waiting to empower and bring each child of God
to his full maturity in Christ.

B. Prov. 16:18 _____

_____

Pride was the sin of Satan. Isa. 14:12 _____

_____

Pride was the first sin of man as Adam and Eve wanted to be
something they were not. Pride is at the root of man's self-
imposed estrangement from God. The self-centered, ego-
centric Christian cannot have fellowship with God: ". . . for
God is opposed to the proud, but gives grace to the hum-
ble" (1 Pet. 5:5).

C. Prov. 29:25 _____

_____

One of the greatest tragedies of our day is the general practice among Christians of conforming to the conduct and
standards of a non-Christian society. Many are afraid to be
different—ashamed to witness for the One "who loved us
and gave Himself for us." Remember, in 1 Peter 2:9 we are
told: _____

_____.

Ps. 147:11 _____

_____.

D. How will Christ feel toward us if we are ashamed of Him? Luke 9:26 _____

_____

Many Christians are fearful of being thought fanatical by their fellow Christians and others should they be filled with the Holy Spirit.

E. What else will put a block between us and the Lord and keep us from being filled with the Spirit? Ps. 66:18

_____

_____

Unconfessed sin keeps many Christians from being filled with the Holy Spirit. Perhaps God has reminded you of a lie you told that has damaged someone's reputation, or "borrowed" merchandise or money that has not been returned, or an unethical transaction, or cheating on an exam, or any number of acts that He wants you to confess to Him. He may lead you to make restitution to those whom you have wronged. Matt. 5:23-24_____

_____

If so, be obedient to His leading. We may be able to hide these sins from our friends and others, but we cannot hide them from God. Ps. 44:21 _____

_____.

Is there anyone whom you have not forgiven? If so, God expects you to forgive them. Mark 11:24-26 _____

_____

However, if we confess these sins to God as the Lord directs us, we are forgiven and cleansed. 1 John 1:9 _____

_____

F. 1 John 2:15-17 _____

_____

A love for material things and a desire to conform to a secular society keep many Christians from being filled with the Holy Spirit. We live a brief span of years and then are gone from this earthly scene. Every Christian should make a careful and frequent evaluation of how he/she invests his/her time, talents, and treasures in order to accomplish the most for the cause of Christ. The poem goes: "Only one life, T'will soon be past; Only what's done for Christ will last." Matt. 6:24,33 _____

_____

_____

G. Lack of trust in God will also keep us from being filled with the Holy Spirit. Read John 3:16 again. Do you feel you could not trust a God like this? _____

_____

Why? Rom. 8:32, 1 John 3:16 _____

_____

_____

This keeps many Christians from making a full surrender of their wills to Him and from being filled with the Holy Spirit. Many Christians have a fear which amounts almost to superstition that, if they surrender themselves fully to God, something tragic will happen to test them. They may fear they will lose a loved one. Some fear that God will send them to some remote section of the world as a missionary to some savage tribe, against their wills.

IV. SUMMARY

The unhappiest people in the world are not the unbelievers, but Christians who resist the will of God for their lives!

LESSON 16

The Fruit of the Spirit   Part I

But the fruit of the Spirit is love, joy, peace, patience, kindness, goodness, faithfulness, gentleness, self-control, against such things there is no law (Gal. 5:22-23).

AIM: To discover the fruit of the Spirit and how it relates to the believer

INTRODUCTION: In Genesis 1:11-12, God declared _____
_____
_____.

And in Genesis 1:23-25*b*, He also stated _____
_____
_____.

The principle suggested is one of "created to produce after its kind." Dawson Trotman, the founder of the Navigators, wrote a booklet titled *Born to Reproduce*. The title suggests that as believers we were not born to produce anything on our own but to reproduce after its kind.

It goes along with the Scriptures listed above and when something reproduces, it has similar characteristics to the original. For example, when you see a lemon tree in Florida, you know it is a lemon tree because of the fruit it has produced on its limbs. It does not seem supernatural that a lemon tree can produce lemons because it was designed to reproduce after its own kind.

In the Christian life, we too are born to reproduce, but what characteristics does or should our tree have in order that others can determine what fruit we are reproducing? Because we are born of the Spirit from above (see John 3) it is expected that we would have His characteristics on our tree. The characteristics are known as the fruit of the Spirit, according to Galatians 5:22-23.

How do we reproduce this fruit? In this lesson we will discuss this question, along with the principles of abiding and pruning, and list the nine expressions of the fruit.

LESSON:

I. HOW DO WE REPRODUCE FRUIT?

Bearing fruit depends a great deal on the type of roots a tree has. According to Psalm 1:2-3, the believer's roots should be planted by _____.

It suggests also that a believer is to meditate upon the Word daily. It is not only essential that a believer have the best roots, but he must also receive the correct nourishment in order to grow. Look up 2 Timothy 3:16-17 and record your observations concerning the nourishment we are to receive. _____

_____

_____

_____

Another key aspect to reproducing fruit is being attached to the right vine in John 15:4-5 _____

_____

_____

From this Scripture we find that people are either remaining in Him or are apart from Him. If they are not connected, no fruit will be produced, for they do not produce it themselves—they just bear it. It is a by-product of being attached to Him.

II. THE WORD AND YOUR LIFE

According to God's Word, there are promises available to believers based upon conditions we must meet. In the following verses, write out the Scripture and then write in your own words the promises we are to receive and the conditions we must meet.

Josh. 1:8 _____

_____

PROMISE _____ CONDITION _____

Ps. 1:2-3 _____

_____

PROMISE _____ CONDITION _____

John 15:7 _____

_____

PROMISE _____ CONDITION _____

III. PRINCIPLE OF ABIDING

The principle of abiding is a prevalent one that runs throughout Scripture. First John has one of the clearest statements concerning abiding. There are several aspects to it as well. In the following Scriptures, observe which aspect of abiding is present in the verse and record your findings below.

1 John 2:6 _____

_____

Aspect of abiding: _____

1 John 2:10 _____

_____

Aspect of abiding: _____

1 John 2:14 _____

_____

Aspect of abiding: _____

1 John 2:17 _____

_____

Aspect of abiding: _____
1 John 3:6 _____

_____

Aspect of abiding: _____
1 John 3:14 _____

_____

Aspect of abiding: _____
1 John 3:24 _____

_____

Aspect of abiding: _____

IV. A PARABLE OF BEARING AND BARRENNESS

In Luke 13:6-9, Jesus shared a parable of the fig tree. The principle involved is bearing or barrenness. God is the owner of the vineyard and when He decides to cut down a fig tree for not bearing, then it's the axe and the fire, for a tree that bears no fruit is worthless in His kingdom. When He takes inventory of your tree, will He find a tree that is bearing fruit or a barren tree? Watch out for the axe!

V. THE PRINCIPLE OF PRUNING

Because a tree bears fruit is no guarantee that it is bearing fruit efficiently. What is necessary is pruning. Pruning cuts back a part of a branch that cuts the strength of the branch to produce more fruit. In the Christian life, what do you think cuts our strength in bearing the fruit of the Spirit? _____

_____

Ask Christ to cut back (prune) your branches so you can produce more fruit to His glory.

VI. THE NINE EXPRESSIONS OF FRUIT

Look up Galatians 5:22-23 and draw a "Christian Tree" that is attached to the "Vine" of Christ and place the nine expressions of fruit on this tree.

VII. SUMMARY

Bearing fruit is a life-long process. The longer you stay hooked to Christ, the more fruit you will bear. On the following chart, determine the stages that a person goes through in life according to John 15:2-5 and record your findings.

much fruit
(John 15:5)

more fruit
(John 15:2)

fruit
(John 15:2)

no fruit
(John 15:2)

Judging yourself on this chart, where would you place yourself? If you are on the first two levels, you need to pray. Ask the Lord to help you to be more open to His Spirit, producing His fruit in your life. Then accept it in faith and practice what you will discover from the following lessons.

LESSON 17

The Fruit of the Spirit   Part II

Now the works of the flesh are these . . . But the fruit of the Spirit is love, joy, peace, patience, kindness, goodness, faithfulness, gentleness, self-control, against such things there is no law (Gal. 5:19, 22,23).

AIM: To discuss the fruit of the Spirit and how it relates to the believer

INTRODUCTION: W. Y. Fullerton writes: "We come to 'the fruit of the Spirit.' It is fruit. You will notice the word is in the singular—not fruits, as we generally say, but fruit; which will emphasize the thought that if there be nine different virtues in this category, it is not that nine different persons are to manifest these virtues, but it is that each person is to have the nine. It is not that one has joy, another peace; but every man has love and joy and peace and all the rest of them."[1]

In John 15:6, Jesus told His disciples, as He was preparing to face the cross, that _____

_____.

Bearing fruit was one of His highest priorities at this point, and He chose them for this specific purpose. They were to be the first examples of the possibility of the supernatural working in the natural. He knew that if the world could see a difference in these men, then it could recognize that His words meant more than mere idle sayings for misfits in society.

Peter seems never to have forgotten this lesson after empowerment of the Spirit, for in 2 Peter 1:5-7, he lists eight blessings that every believer should experience. Write out these verses in your own words below.

_____

_____

_____

_____

In this lesson we will discuss the contrasts and differences between the works of the flesh versus the fruit of the Spirit. Be open to the Spirit as He speaks to you concerning experiencing the fruit of the Spirit.

LESSON:

I. CONTRASTS OF WORKS OF THE FLESH WITH THE FRUIT OF THE SPIRIT

In Galatians 5:19-21, Paul lists seventeen manifestations of the works of the flesh. It is not a complete list, for no one knows all of the darkness that can emerge from a heart entrenched in itself.

The contrasting of the fruit of the Spirit with the works of the flesh delivers a sharp distinction as to the beauty the Spirit can provide and the deprivation the flesh can produce. There are four types of sins listed in the works of the flesh. They are:

"(1) Sins of misdirected physical desire—in the realm of sex

(2) Sins of misdirected faith—in the realm of religion

(3) Violations of brotherly love—in the realm of society

(4) Sins of excess—in the realm of drink."[2]

The works of the flesh listed in Galatians 5 far outnumber those of the Spirit's fruit. A. R. Foussett stated, "It is proof of our fallen state, how much richer every vocabulary is in words for sin than those for graces." In your life, do you know more concerning the works of the flesh or the fruit of the Spirit? Your perspective of living life will determine which you know more about and which you desire more of. What is your choice? Write it down now. _____

II. WORKS OF THE FLESH VERSUS FRUIT OF THE SPIRIT—PLURAL VERSUS SINGULAR

In Galatians 5, Paul makes an obvious contrast concerning works and fruit. The works of the flesh are different acts of deprivation performed by man. The fruit of the Spirit is one aspect of the life in the Spirit that produces nine different expressions.

Paul uses the singular fruit to emphasize that all the Spirit produces in the life of a believer is unified and coherent, while the works of the flesh produce nothing but disharmony and instability, not only within a person, but in his relationship with others.

Man cannot produce or manufacture the fruit of the Spirit at any price, for it is beyond his realm of understanding that the fruit is not based upon self—but upon the Savior. Therefore, no amount of imitation can produce the supernatural influences of the Spirit. The fruit of the Spirit is not necessarily what we do but what we are.

III. SUMMARY

The nine expressions of the fruit of the Spirit are grouped together into three separate groups. The first group deals with the believer in his relationship to God (discussed in Lessons 18-20), the second treats the believer in his relationship to others (discussed in Lessons 21-23), and the third group talks about the believer in relationship to himself (discussed in Lessons 24-26). The fruit is manifested in the realm of experience, in the realm of conduct, and in the realm of character.

LESSON 18

The Fruit of the Spirit   Part III

Love

And the fruit of the Spirit is love (Gal. 5:22a).

AIM: To discuss specifically the fruit of love and how it relates to the believers

INTRODUCTION: Jesus has all of the different qualities of the fruit of the Spirit to the level of perfection. Because they are in His life, we who are His children by faith should have them as well. Ephesians 3:19 states that we are "to know, by experience,

_____,

in order that we _____."

1 Peter 1:8 suggests that in spite of not having seen Jesus in bodily form, we should _____.

In this lesson, we will give a biblical definition of the word love and present practical examples of how this love is and should be expressed.

LESSON:

I. LOVE

The word love comes from the Greek word *agape* which means an unconditional expression of seeking the highest good for the object of our affection. Love is the first quality listed in Galatians 5:22a because the remaining qualities are different forms of love. There are three Greek words that are translated into our one word love. They are:

(1) *Eros* that refers to a sexual type of love and is not found in the New Testament,

(2) *Philos* which is a brotherly type of love for all mankind,

(3) *Agape* which is God's constant expression of affection toward unworthy man. According to 1 Corinthians 13:8

_____

_____

_____ ,

this type of love never fails.

Jesus declared in John 13:34-35 _____

_____

_____ ,

that all men will know that we are His disciples, not by how we preach, not by how beautifully we sing, and not by how much we give, but by the only quality that cannot be duplicated in the world, love.

Even John 3:16 suggests that God's explanation of sending Christ to die on the cross was because of love, _____

_____ .

Jesus' commandment that is echoed throughout the New Testament is found in John 15:13 _____

_____ .

II. EXAMPLES OF LOVE, GOD-STYLE

Someone has observed that "love can be known only from the action it prompts!" Look up the following verses and record the actions by God that show He loves us. Record your findings below.

Rom. 5:8 _____

_____

John 3:16 _____

_____

1 John 4:19-21 _____

Rom. 5:5

Eph. 2:4

1 John 4:10

The following verses suggest ways of how we can share the *agape* love that we are to demonstrate. Look them up and record the principles that we are to display.

John 14:21

Eph. 4:15

1 John 5:3

Matt. 19:19

John 15:12

1 John 3:16-18

III. SUMMARY

The Holy Spirit goes much further than the sensual *eros* or the brotherly *philos* but all the way to *agape*. He produces in the life of every willing believer God's type of expression toward mankind. This even includes our enemies for the purpose of winning them to Christ. If you expressed this type of love to your enemies, would it make a difference in their lives?

As Romans 5:8 states, God demonstrated His love toward us

that while we were unlovable, He allowed His most lovable Son to come and die on a horrible cross for our sins. Doing what needed to be done in spite of how He felt is the key to expressing God's type of love to our family or to our enemies. We cannot produce this; neither is it native to our character. It must come from the Spirit within us as He produces it. It is more than emotions or feelings. It is doing and acting. Therefore, love is an act of one's will.

LESSON 19

The Fruit of the Spirit   Part IV

Joy

And the fruit of the Spirit is love, joy, . . . (Gal. 5:22*a*).

AIM: To discuss specifically the fruit of joy and how it relates to the believer

INTRODUCTION: Joy is often used synonymously with happiness. Biblically the two words do not mean the same thing. Happiness occurs when our circumstances match our expectations. According to 1 Thessalonians 1:6, joy is the result of the inward reality of the Holy Spirit. It supercedes our circumstances and has no limitations. Neh. 8:10 _____

_____

_____,

states that "the joy of the Lord is our strength." When we need strength to go on living this life, strength is only an experience away. Jesus also taught that what He had spoken to us would expand our joy beyond what it is already. John 15:11 _____

_____

The believers who have an intimate relationship with Christ will find their joy in Him and not in happenings or things. In this lesson we will define the quality of joy and some practical examples of joy according to the Word of God.

LESSON:

I. JOY

The word joy comes from the Greek word *chara*, which means a joy grounded in a sincere relationship to God. This quality of character is produced only by the Spirit. Because of its spiritual source, joy can co-exist with sorrow. Refer to 2 Corinthians 6:10 _____

_____

_____.

Paul writes in Romans 14:17 that the kingdom itself is not based on the temporal, perishable things but "righteousness, and peace, and _____"
There is a paradox to the type of spiritual joy that the Spirit produces in the lives of believers. It can be experienced in the middle of turbulent persecution, as with the Thessalonians. Paul wrote of them in 1 Thessalonians 1:6 _____

_____

_____.

Jesus Himself is referred to in Isaiah 53:3 as a "man of sorrows and acquainted with grief," but Hebrews 1:9 states that "God has _____."
What do you think is the difference between happiness and joy?

The Scriptures will provide profound insight concerning the differences. Use a biblical concordance and look up all of the references to the word joy and its other forms. Then look up all of the references to happiness and its other forms. Make observations concerning each reference as to its context and implied meaning. Then compare your findings and record them below.

Reference	Meaning	Reference	Meaning

How visible should this experience of spiritual joy be? _____

_____

_____

II. SUMMARY

Philippians is a splendid Book about how to have joy in the midst of troubles. It was written by Paul while he was in prison, and yet it was one of his most joyful letters. It shows that joy is not dependent upon present circumstances. Only the Holy Spirit can produce such an experience that transcends circumstances.

What reaction do you receive from Paul's admonition to "rejoice in the Lord *always*"? _____

_____

_____

LESSON 20

The Fruit of the Spirit   Part V

Peace

And the fruit of the Spirit is love, joy, peace, . . . (Gal. 5:22a).

AIM: To discuss specifically the fruit of peace and how it relates to the believer

INTRODUCTION: Peace is a word misunderstood by believers and non-believers alike. Some consider the meaning to be the absence of war. Biblically speaking, peace is that quiet assurance which operates in either war or calm. To possess this type of peace, it starts with peace with God. Paul prayed that the Philippians would know the peace that passes all understanding.

In this lesson we will define the quality of peace and give practical examples of experiencing this virtue.

LESSON:

I. PEACE

The word peace comes from the Greek word *eirené,* which means at ease, calmness underneath the skin. It is enjoyed only by the believers who are living in conformity to His will. In John 14:27, Jesus said that the very thing most people are seeking, He is leaving for us to accept. _____

_____

_____

We have to accept Him as Lord and Savior first and live according to His will before we can experience this *peace.* According to Philippians 4:7 _____ this same peace will keep cares and concerns from destroying the serenity that He gives. It is not only experienced in circumstances that are favorable, but is a supernatural aspect produced by the Spirit Who operates under any circumstances.

Worry often reveals a lack of inner peace. Jesus has some suggestions concerning worries and peace in Matthew 6:25-34. Determine your answer to the following questions from studying the above passage. Record your answers below.

What are some of the general kinds of concerns that cause people to worry? _____

_____

_____

_____

What attitudes or actions cause us to worry? _____

_____

_____

_____

According to Matthew 6:32, how does worry reflect on God's character? _____

_____

_____

What is the scriptural solution that will give us peace within?

_____

_____

_____

_____

II. SUMMARY

Read Philippians 4:6-8 and observe which things are bothering you and stealing your peace. Record your findings below.

_____

_____

_____

_____

_____

Pray about the things you have listed above and do so in thanksgiving, using Proverbs 3:5,6 as your support.

Look at verse 9 in Philippians 4 and compare it with Isaiah 26:3 in the KJV. What are the similarities between these two verses? Record your observations below.

_____

_____

_____

_____

_____

Take an inventory of your thought life and determine if your thoughts have short-circuited your inner peace. Ask Christ for a renewed mind according to Romans 12:2, _____

_____ ,

and for His mind to be in you according to Philippians 2:5

_____

_____

_____

_____

_____ .

LESSON 21

The Fruit of the Spirit   Part VI

Patience

And the fruit of the Spirit is love, joy, peace, patience, . . ." (Gal. 5:22).

AIM: To discuss specifically the fruit of patience and how it relates to the believer

INTRODUCTION: Patience is almost foreign to Western culture. People expect everything in an instant, and provisions are made to avoid delays or discomforts. Patience is biblically associated with trials and tribulations and implies an underlying strength of a soul while remaining under stress. Patience results in endurance to experience stresses and struggles in life. This virtue can only be produced by the Holy Spirit.

In this lesson we will define the quality of patience and give practical examples of experiencing this virtue.

LESSON:

I. PATIENCE

The word patience comes from the Greek word *makrothumia* which comes from the two Greek root words *makros*, which means long, and *thumos*, which means temper. "Long temper" is exactly what patience involves. The KJV translates this as "longsuffering." The Greek word suggests a person's steadfastness under provocation.

The context of the word involves having patience toward people who can and will aggravate or persecute others. It also suggests a slowness to avenge wrongs suffered or a refusal to retaliate. According to Exodus 34:6 _____

_____

_____,

this fruit is associated as an attribute of God. It's good that God has this character quality, but we are to have this quality as well. Jesus set an example of having patience in 1 Peter 2:23, where Peter writes _____

_____.

Sometimes patience is linked with testing or trials. Other characteristics may also be involved. Look up James 1:2-3 and write down your observations about God's tests. What characteristic is involved? _____

_____

_____

_____

II. SUMMARY

Fruit demonstrates itself in actions, attitudes, and ambitions. It is also accompanied by Christ's attitudes. List the attitudes and actions that are expected from believers who follow Him.

PASSAGE	ATTITUDE	ACTION
1 Pet. 5:5		
Rom. 12:10		
1 Cor. 12:25		

Luke 8:15 suggests that if we take in the Word, it will bring forth fruit with patience. From this we can gather that our lives will involve working *out* what His Word and Spirit have worked *in*. Look up 2 Peter 1:5-8 and observe which qualities are based upon the fruit of the Spirit that should be in your life. After meditating upon them, write down your responses below.

_____

_____

_____

_____

_____

_____

LESSON 22

The Fruit of the Spirit   Part VII

Kindness

And the fruit of the Spirit is love, joy, peace, patience, kindness, . . . (Gal. 5:22).

AIM: To discuss specifically the fruit of kindness and how it relates to the believer

INTRODUCTION: In the second cluster of fruit that the Spirit produces in the lives of believers is kindness (or gentleness in the KJV). It is an action of love that never fails. In this lesson we will define the quality of kindness and give practical examples of experiencing this virtue.

LESSON:

I. KINDNESS

The word kindness comes from the Greek word *chrestotes,* which means serviceable, good. In the KJV it is translated "gentleness." According to J. B. Lightfoot, kindness is a good disposition towards one's neighbors, or kindliness. As with patience, it expresses God's attitude towards people. According to Ephesians 2:12, God saves us in order that _____ _____.

Titus 3:4 suggests that our kindness is to be a reflection of the same kindness and love that He showered on us through Christ. It is a powerful source that is in reserve with the option of using it when needed. God has this same quality of kindness, and His resources are plentiful. His Spirit has given us this same characteristic.

91

Paul admonishes us by the *meekness* and *kindness* of Christ
in 2 Corinthians 10:1a. Using this as our guide ought to produce in us 2 Timothy 2:24b _____

_____.

According to Jeremiah 32:18, what can you learn concerning the kindness of the Lord? Record your observations below.
Compare this with Isaiah 63:7a.

_____

_____

_____

II. SUMMARY

One of the duties of a believer who serves the Lord is to ex-
hibit kindness. How does a believer demonstrate this quality?
Record your answer below.

_____

_____

_____

_____

Fruit demonstrates itself in actions, attitudes, and ambitions. It
is also accompanied by Christ's attitudes. List the attitudes and
actions that are expected from believers who follow Him.

PASSAGE	ATTITUDE	ACTION
James 4:11	_____	_____
Col. 3:9	_____	_____
Gal. 5:15	_____	_____

LESSON 23

The Fruit of the Spirit   Part VIII

Goodness

And the fruit of the Spirit is love, joy, peace, patience, kindness, goodness, . . . (Gal. 5:22).

AIM: To discuss specifically the fruit of goodness and how it relates to the believer

INTRODUCTION: Scripture uses the analogy of a marriage concerning our walk with Christ. In Romans 7:4-6, Paul writes

_____

_____

_____.

This validates the special relationship we have with Him and with each other. Jesus prayed that all believers would be John 17:20,21 _____

_____

_____.

Having a spirit of oneness is designed to produce the fruit He desires for us to possess, in order that the world might know God loves mankind and that He sent Jesus to die for their sins.

Man has always produced some sort of fruit. Usually it is fruit unto death. Now with the Spirit, we have the opportunity to produce fruit unto God and life. In this lesson, we will define the quality of goodness and give practical examples of experiencing this virtue.

LESSON:

I. GOODNESS

According to Vines, the word "goodness" comes from the Greek word *agathosune* which comes from the root word *agathos,* an adjective describing something which, being good in its character or constitution, is beneficial in its effect. It represents God's highest standards and is evidenced in favorable actions toward all others it comes into contact with. It is no respecter of persons.

When this virtue is produced in the life of a believer, it will not only influence his attitude toward his relationship to God and his standards, but also his activity and ambitions toward persons. As a result of demonstrating this "goodness," others will want to experience it too.

"Goodness" has been called by Dr. A. Z. Conrad, "an abandoned waif—neglected, abused, misunderstood. Of royal blood, yet snubbed, sneered at and avoided. Highest and holiest in the category of virtues, yet disowned and undesired. Call a young man 'good' and he will resent the occasion and proceed to demonstrate that he has been falsely accused, by engaging in some wild adventure."

Goodness is active in experience and not passive. It is also practical. Jesus Himself was characteristically good, as recorded in Acts 10:38 _____

_____

_____.

The believer, if living under the influence of the Spirit, will imitate his Master according to Ephesians 5:9 _____

_____

_____.

This characteristic of an inward quality that manifests itself in outward actions is more than a kindly disposition, but such that is like Dorcas in Acts 9:36 _____

_____

_____.

II. SUMMARY

When we consider the fruit of the Spirit, our study reveals a great deal about the Spirit Himself. He reproduces His qualities in our lives in order that non-believers can see God in us. Psalm 33:5 states that the whole earth is full of His goodness. All we have to do is look around. Yet when the world looks at us, does it also see His goodness? Look at Romans 2:4 and record your insights concerning the goodness of the Lord and how far it will reach. _____

_____

_____

_____

Fruit demonstrates itself in actions, attitudes, and ambitions. It is also accompanied by Christ's attitudes. List the attitudes and actions that are expected from believers who follow Him.

PASSAGE	ATTITUDE	ACTION
Heb. 3:13		
1 Thess. 4:18		

LESSON 24

The Fruit of the Spirit   Part IX

Faithfulness

And the fruit of the Spirit is love, joy, peace, patience, kindness, goodness, faithfulness, . . . (Gal. 5:22-23).

AIM: To discuss specifically the fruit of faithfulness and how it relates to the believer

INTRODUCTION: *Faithfulness* is a character quality linked with gentleness and self-control. What I *am* as a believer determines what I *do* as a believer. If I do not live a life that expresses a holy character, then the fruit of the Spirit is not operating in my life. *Faithfulness* helps me to be true to the One who has called me from a life of sin unto salvation. In this lesson we will define what faithfulness is, determine what a lack of faithfulness is, delineate tests of faithfulness, and describe the quality of faithfulness God expects of us.

LESSON:

I. FAITHFULNESS

The word faithfulness comes from the Greek word *pistos* which means "to be trusted, loyal, or expressing fidelity." It comes from the same Greek word as "faith," which means a firm persuasion or a conviction based upon hearing. The idea of faithfulness is that the Spirit produces in the life of the believer the character quality of loyalty based upon a firm persuasion about a conviction concerning Christ.

It is a product of a continued loyalty towards God by saying "yes." Our loyalty to Him is not dependent upon us, but on His loyalty to us. 2 Timothy 2:13 states _____

_____

_____,

which means that if we fail Him, He will still remain faithful. We could never outdo His faithfulness. Lamentations 3:22-23 states _____

_____

_____.

His mercies and faithfulness are new each day.

II. OF WHAT VALUE IS FIDELITY?

Fidelity is a virtue commended in Scripture. It is a test of character, as Jesus indicated in Matthew 25:21 _____

_____.

The same quality is suggested in 2 Peter 2:21-22 _____

_____

_____,

and in 3 John 12 _____

_____.

III. A LACK OF FAITHFULNESS

Sometimes in our walk with Christ we become lax in our loyalty to Him. If it becomes a regular habit, it could be a sign of spiritual immaturity. Some teenagers, and adults as well, display signs of emotional immaturity by refusing to accept responsibilities. Fathers refuse to take responsibility for their children. Yet, not doing so negates being a mature father. This too occurs in the realm of the spirit, when responsibilities God has given us go left undone because of disobedience. We are then unfaithful and disloyal to Him. However, when we accept these responsibilities, then we are truly faithful and show our loyalty.

IV. THE TESTS OF FAITHFULNESS

There are three basic tests that can determine our faithfulness to Christ and His kingdom. They are:

1. How much time we spend reading His Word;
2. How much time we spend praying to Him; and
3. How much we live for Him when He has blessed us with prosperity.

Now take these tests and record your answers below.

_____

_____

_____

V. SUMMARY

Too many times in our lives we become overwhelmed by the expectations that God desires of us. However, it is essential to remind ourselves of what we can expect from Him. Meditate about the quality of faithfulness and how it relates to the following expectations:

FRUIT	WHAT I CAN EXPECT FROM GOD	WHAT GOD EXPECTS FROM ME
FAITHFULNESS	Rev. 2:10 Luke 16:10-12	Lam. 3:22-23 1 Thess. 5:24 2 Tim. 2:13
	_____	_____
	_____	_____
	_____	_____
	_____	_____

When most people think of faithfulness, it is usually in the context of large tasks with great responsibilities. Jesus was more concerned with how "faithful" we are in the little things He assigns to us. Look up Luke 16:10-12 and record your list of the "little" which Jesus has asked us to be faithful in. _____

_____

_____

_____

_____

_____

According to Matthew 25:21, what promise has He made to us if we prove ourselves faithful in the "little" things? _____

_____

_____

"Pentecost resulted in an astounding transformation in the character of the disciples in respect to faithfulness. Only a few days previously they had all proved faithless to their Master and had left Him to suffer and die alone, forsaken by God and man. But when filled with the Spirit, they proved faithful under the most fearful persecution. Some were 'faithful unto death,' and received the 'well done!' reserved by the Master for the good and faithful servant."[1] What about you? Are you faithful where it counts?

LESSON 25

The Fruit of the Spirit   Part X

Gentleness

And the fruit of the Spirit is love, joy, peace, patience, kindness, goodness, faithfulness, gentleness . . . (Gal. 5:22-23).

AIM: To discover the fruit of gentleness and how it relates to the believer

INTRODUCTION: The fruit of *gentleness* (meekness) is perhaps the least desired of the qualities the Spirit produces in our lives. Some people confuse meekness with weakness and almost treat this virtue as a quality to be avoided. Far from being weak, gentleness is a quiet sense of the adequacy that comes from being brought under the control of the Spirit, like a wild horse that has been broken. Tremendous power is resident, yet it is harnessed to do the best good. When a person's spirit can be brought under control as to release the energy of the Spirit in his life, then that person is experiencing the fruit of *gentleness*.

LESSON:

I. GENTLENESS

The word gentleness comes from the Greek word *prautes* meaning "gentle submissiveness." Jesus taught in Matthew 5:5

_____

_____

_____.

This sheds light on the quality of gentleness (meekness). Happy are the gentle or meek for they will inherit the earth.

"Inherit" carries the idea of handing down from one generation to another. Happiness comes into play while the believer practices the qualities of gentleness. The believer may not inherit his Father's resources immediately, but the day will come when the Father will turn over His resources to the gentle.

In Scripture, this word does not include the idea of being spiritless and timid. The illustration of a wild horse is useful to us at this point. A gentle/meek person is as a wild horse under control. Until he/she is brought under control by the Holy Spirit, they will be unable to present effectively a balanced Spirit-filled life-style. Peter is a good example of before-and-after qualities. Before the presence of the Spirit in his life, Peter was impulsive and temperamental. Yet when the Spirit took control, his life made a radical change for Christ.

Moses was called the meekest man, yet he too was like Peter until God placed a special call upon his life. Even after Moses' call, God had to use forty years in the desert before Moses submitted to His control of his life. A river under the right control can produce power for many. A fire under the right control can also produce warmth to heat a home. Gentleness/meekness is the same kind of power, strength, spirit—wildness under control. It also has the qualities of being sensitive toward others.

II. DEFINITION OF GENTLENESS (MEEKNESS)

Gentleness is referred to as love under discipline. David Hubbard says that gentleness/meekness is making ourselves consistently available to those who count on us; as a result we are at peace with our power, so we do not use it arrogantly or hurtfully. T. DeWitt Talmadge wrote, "As the heavens prophetically are taken by violence, so the earth is taken by meekness, and God as proprietor wants no tenants more or grants large leases than to the meek of heart and spirit."

An iceberg is also an illustration of gentleness. When we view an iceberg, we normally see only 10 percent of the total mass. The other 90 percent is hidden from view. They are dangerous to all ships on the seas, but they have one enemy, the sun. It can melt the most massive iceberg known. The same with the human body, soul, and spirit. Gentleness is as powerful as the sun in dealing with believers. It permits God's character of gentleness to work on our iceberg hearts, changing them into useful instruments under his control.

III. HOW TO APPLY GENTLENESS

According to Billy Graham, in his book *The Holy Spirit*, we can apply gentleness through three avenues. "Jesus set before us His own example by calling upon us to be in Matthew 11:29

_____

_____

_____ .

A. Do not rise up defensively when our feelings are ruffled, as Peter did when he cut off the ear of a soldier at the arrest of Jesus in the garden, only earning His Lord's rebuke (Matt. 25:51,52 _____

_____

_____).

B. Do not crave to have the preeminence as Diotrophes did in 3 John 9 _____

_____

_____ .

Rather, desire that in all things Jesus Christ might have the preeminence (Col. 1:18 _____

_____).

C. Do not seek to be recognized and highly regarded, or to be considered the voice of authority, as Jannes and Jambres did (2 Tim. 3:8 _____

_____)."[1]

IV. SUMMARY

Too many times in our lives we become overwhelmed by the expectations that God desires of us. However, it is essential to remind ourselves of what we can expect from Him. Meditate about the quality of gentleness and how it relates to the following expectations:

FRUIT	WHAT I CAN EXPECT FROM GOD	WHAT GOD EXPECTS FROM ME
GENTLENESS	Titus 3:2 James 1:21 1 Pet. 3:15	Matt. 11:28,29 Matt. 5:5
	_____	_____
	_____	_____
	_____	_____
	_____	_____
	_____	_____

LESSON 26

The Fruit of the Spirit   Part XI

Self-Control

And the fruit of the Spirit is love, joy, peace, patience, kindness, goodness, faithfulness, gentleness, self-control, against such things there is no law (Gal. 5:22-23).

AIM: To discover the last fruit of the Spirit—self-control, and how it relates to the believer

INTRODUCTION: Related to gentleness (meekness) is self-control. Proverbs 25:28 says _____

_____.

Self-control carries the idea of having strength over thoughts and actions. When the world is spreading uncontrolled lust and greed at every turn, there is a severe need for the believer to demonstrate this gift. If the world is ever to come under the controlling influence of the Spirit, believers are to lead the way. When the world sees our self-control then, according to 1 Peter 3:15 _____

_____,

they will ask the reason of the hope that is within us, and when we talk, it will coincide with our Spirit-filled, self-controlled lifestyle.

LESSON:

I. SELF-CONTROL

Self-control (translated temperance in the KJV) comes from the Greek word *enkrateia*, which comes from the root word *kra-*

tos, meaning strength. Vines states that "temperance is . . . one form of self-control; the powers bestowed by God . . . are capable of abuse; the right use demands the controlling power of the will under the operation of the Spirit of God." The word conveys the meaning today of being able to control one's thought life and actions. This character quality separates human from animal. Paul gives an illustration of self-control in 1 Corinthians 9:25, when he states _____

_____

_____.

Junk food, liquor, and other indulgences were avoided because they could hinder the contestant as a participant in the games. We too are in a type of training that is spiritual, and what we allow to affect us in training will show up when we are running in the race. According to 1 Corinthians 9:27 _____

_____

_____,

Paul states that we are to bring our bodies under subjection because there is the danger that if we do not, we will suffer the very things we preach against (become castaways).

Self-control is not done by the energy of the flesh, but it is a fruit of the Spirit that comes from within and affects the outside. It is not the control of self by self. In Ephesians 5:18, _____

_____

_____,

Paul compares the self-control of the Spirit-filled believer with the excesses of an alcoholic. For believers, self-control carries an idea of the subjection of our life in every area to the penetrating presence of the Spirit within.

In Galatians 5:16-18 _____

_____

_____

_____,

Paul portrays this human struggle.

II. SUMMARY

"'The fruit of the Spirit is love.' Only as we live in love can we fulfill the will of God in our lives. The believer must become love-inspired, love-mastered, and love-driven (2 Cor. 5:14 _
_____).
Without the fruit of the Spirit (love), we are just a religious noise (1 Cor. 13:1 _____

_____

_____).

'The fruit of the Spirit is love,' and it is manifested in joy, peace, patience, kindness, goodness, faithfulness, gentleness, and self-control:

(1) Joy is love's strength
(2) Peace is love's security
(3) Patience is love's longsuffering
(4) Kindness is love's conduct
(5) Goodness is love's character
(6) Faithfulness is love's confidence
(7) Gentleness is love's humility
(8) Self-control is love's victory
      'Against such there is no law.'

A Holy Spirit-controlled man needs no law to cause him to live a righteous life. The secret of a Spirit-controlled life is found in dedication to God (Rom. 12:1-2 _____

_____

_____).

Put your all on the altar, and the Holy Spirit will fill your heart with the love of God" (Rom. 5:5 _____

_____

_____).[1]

LESSON 27

The Gifts of the Spirit   Part I

And since we have gifts that differ according to the grace given to us, let each exercise them accordingly . . . if prophecy, according to the proportion of his faith; if service, in his serving; or he who teaches, in his teaching; or he who exhorts, in his exhortation; he who gives, with liberality; he who leads, with diligence; he who shows mercy, with cheerfulness (Rom. 12: 6-8, cf. 1 Cor. 12:8-10, cf. Eph. 4:11).

AIM: To introduce the doctrine (teaching) on the gifts of the Spirit to the believer

INTRODUCTION: This is the first lesson in a series of twenty-one lessons on discovering the gifts of the Spirit. By way of introduction, there are many gifts the Spirit can give us as believers. They are given at the moment of our conversion, and sometimes they are never developed to the point of actual use. The reason: many believers do not know that they have a gift(s) or they do not know what gift(s) they have.

Through this introduction we will share some insights as to: what kinds of gifts exist, do we all have a gift, what assurance do we have of knowing we have a gift, and, since God has given me a gift(s), what can I give to Him in return?

LESSON:

I. WHAT KINDS OF GIFTS ARE THERE?

There are three categories of spiritual gifts.

1. Motivational gifts found in Romans 12:3-8,

2. Ministry gifts found in 1 Corinthians 12:27-31 and
   Ephesians 4:11, and
3. Manifestation gifts found in 1 Corinthians 2:7-11.

In order to become better acquainted with the different gifts the Spirit can give, read the following three passages and list each gift.

Romans 12:6-8   1 Corinthians 12:8-10   Ephesians 4:11

_____   _____   _____

_____   _____   _____

_____   _____   _____

_____   _____   _____

_____   _____   _____

_____   _____   _____

How do we recognize our gifts in order to develop them? There are four principles we need to follow in order to find and develop our gift(s).

First, we need to settle in our hearts that He has indeed given us a gift(s). Once you have settled this and are assured He will not deceive you concerning this, spend time in prayer and study of the Word to find out the characteristics and responsibilities of each gift.

Second, we need to become involved in some area of ministry where we can observe, and others as well, what our gift is or is not. When God gives us a gift(s), we will not be the only person who knows we have it. Others will notice it too.

Third, we then need to seek out opportunities among believers in order to develop and exercise the gift(s) we have discovered. We also should prepare to wait for some results of exercising our gifts. The end result will be a ministry God has given to us.

Last, we must keep in mind the importance of the Giver over the gift(s). We need to know more about Him, and He will reveal more of His grace to us.

II. THE ASSURANCE OF A GIFT(S)

In Romans 8:32, Paul states _____

_____

_____.

This informs us that since He was not willing to spare His own Son, He is also willing to give us freely all things necessary for us to live this live and please Him in doing His will. Giving us spiritual gifts is included in this.

According to 1 Corinthians 2:12, Paul teaches basically the same concept _____

_____

_____.

From these Scriptures we realize that God is willing to give to us exactly what we need in order to operate according to His divine blueprint. This assurance is as trustworthy as the Word of God itself.

III. GIFTS INCUR PRIVILEGES AS WELL AS RESPONSIBILITIES

When we receive a gift from the Spirit, we also receive the privilege to use it, as well as the responsibility to use it according to His will. First Peter 4:10-11 states that our responsibilities in relation to our gifts are _____

_____

_____

_____.

Another Scripture relating to our responsibilities is Ephesians 4:16, which says _____

_____

_____.

But sometimes this fails, due to a principle found in 1 Corinthians 12:14-22. Write down your observations as to what principle we violate in our responsibilities. _____

_____

_____

_____

IV. GIVING IN RETURN TO GOD

From our perspective as believers, we are always receiving from God. Yet there is another side to the relationship. We can give to Him. Look up the following verses and list what we can give to God.

2 Cor. 8:5 _____

_____

Prov. 23:26 _____

_____

Rom. 12:1,2 _____

_____

1 Thess. 5:18 _____

_____

1 Tim. 4:13-15 _____

_____

Rev. 14:7 _____

_____

Matt. 23:23_____

_____

V. SUMMARY

There are numerous gifts that the Spirit gives to believers. In the next twenty lessons, we will look into each gift specifically and see how it relates to the believer. For further study, write down in your own words a description of the characteristics and qualifications of each gift. Start with Ephesians 4:11 and use a Bible dictionary to gain a clearer understanding of each gift. From a practical standpoint, observe someone who is exercising the gift you think the Spirit has given to you. Also try to receive counsel and confirmation concerning your gift as well.

LESSON 28

The Gifts of the Spirit   Part II

And since we have gifts that differ according to the grace given to us, let each exercise them accordingly; if prophecy, according to the proportion of his faith; if service, in his serving; or he who teaches, in his teaching; or he who exhorts, he who leads, with diligence; he who shows mercy, with cheerfulness (Rom. 12:6-8, cf. 1 Cor. 12:8-10, cf. Eph. 4:11).

AIM: To introduce the doctrine (teaching) on the gifts of the Spirit to the believer

INTRODUCTION: Growing up in a farm community, I experienced many holidays together with relatives. It was a warm, loving, family community. At Christmas, all the children came together to open up presents and see what one another had received. Joy and excitement filled the room. Later, after the newness of the gifts had worn off, jealousy and squabbling began. This is also true of spiritual gifts. Sometimes believers who are not as mature as others become a little jealous when they realize they do not have a particular prominent gift.

Sometimes those with prominent gifts may have a spirit of pride and superiority. However, when the gifts were given, the Spirit did so based on the needs and call of God for a believer's life. In the above Scriptures, there are three passages listing the "gifts of the Spirit"—Romans 12:6-8, 1 Corinthians 12:8-10, and Ephesians 4:11.

LESSON:

I. GIFTS AND THE BODY

In 1 Corinthians 12:4-7 _____

_____

_____

_____,

we are taught that every believer is given at least one gift by the Spirit. God holds us responsible for how we use our gifts. In 1 Corinthians 12:14-27, Paul compares the Church with our bodies. He adds that even those members which have seemingly insignificant responsibilities are necessities in God's body for proper functioning. Some members may have the same gift, yet there is so much uniqueness in the kingdom which makes each of us distinct in our use of our gifts.

II. THE MEANING OF CHARISMA (GIFT)

Paul uses the Greek word *charisma* (plural *charismata*) to refer to the gifts that God gives His believers through His Spirit. The plural form of the word is found only in Paul's writings. It means "manifestations of grace" and is translated "gifts." There are two other words Paul uses to refer to "gifts." They are found in Ephesians 4 and are the Greek words *dorea* and *doma*. Another word also used is *pneumatika,* which means "things that belong to the Spirit." All these different words mean about the same thing.

III. THE ORIGIN OF SPIRITUAL GIFTS

What is the origin of spiritual gifts? They come from the Holy Spirit, and He makes the decision as to who receives which gifts. With the gift(s) that we receive, we are held responsible for their use. We may desire other gifts and may even petition the Spirit for them, but if it is not His will, we will not receive them. If we become ungrateful because the Spirit does not give us the gift we seem to want, we sin against Him.

We have discussed in earlier lessons the fruit of the Spirit, and we have shown that the fruit of the Spirit should be characteristic in the life of every believer, but not every believer will have the same gifts as every other believer.

IV. SPIRITUAL GIFTS AND TALENTS

In studying the three passages we have outlined earlier, we find a total of twenty gifts. There are additional gifts listed in the Old Testament as well. Most of these gifts, however, seem to be similar to natural talents or abilities. Others that are listed were already spiritual in character.

Is there a difference between spiritual gifts and natural talents? One person may have the talent of making beautiful children's clothes; another may have a talent for music. In reality, many people have natural talents and abilities of one kind or another, and these too come from God.

The problem is equating spiritual gifts with natural talents. This is an error that needs to be corrected. The two are not synonymous. Believers and unbelievers may have skills which, with development, can become highly developed. *These, however are not gifts of the Spirit.* Neither do they become gifts of the Spirit if a person becomes a Christian. They are still human talents, even though they may be committed to the Lord's service.

A gift of the Spirit is a manifestation of service through a believer. It is a tool or an instrument not used for personal enjoyment alone. It has been given to believers for use in the functioning of the body of Christ. In Exodus 31:3-5, we read

_____

_____

_____

_____.

From this text, we discover that many of the skills and talents people have are gifts of God. The abilities of Bezalel, which were given by the Spirit, included manual ability as well as intellectual wisdom and understanding, which is necessary in all art.

This too comes from God as stated in James 1:17 _____
_____
_____.

God has given humans artistic abilities which were corrupted in the fall. Though they were corrupted, they are still present.

Therefore, the difference between spiritual gifts and natural talents is that spiritual gifts are given to serve and minister to the body. Natural talents are legitimate abilities, yet they are not specifically designed for ministering to saints or sinners. That is why the same person with a talent for singing can sing in the church and the night club at the same time without ministering to either.

V. PURPOSE OF GIFTS

As stated by Paul in Ephesians 4:12, the purpose of spiritual gifts is _____
_____.

In other words, God has given each of us a task to do and the gifts to perform that task. If we fail to perform this task, we face His disapproval at the "judgment seat of Christ." All believers will one day face Christ and give an account of the work done in our flesh, which includes the use of the gifts He has given us. In the Greek, the judgment seat is the term *bema,* found in 2 Corinthians 5:10 _____
_____
_____.

This will not be a judgment of sins but a decision of the value of our work for the kingdom. Our sins have been dealt with by the blood of Christ, and we will enter heaven, regardless of the quantity or quality of our works. 1 Corinthians 3:11-15 states
_____
_____
_____

_____

_____.

Are you using your gifts to build items of gold, silver, and precious stones, or are you using wood, hay, and stubble? The results will be rewards or loss.

In 1 Corinthians 12:7, Paul states that gifts were given for

_____

_____.

As a result, we are not to use them selfishly but to help one another. In Philippians 2:3-4, Paul also says _____

_____

_____.

God has also given us the ability to help "unite" the body of Christ through the Spirit. In Ephesians 4:3-7, Paul admonished us to be _____

_____

_____.

As a result, we are never to divide the body of Christ but to unify it.

VI. SUMMARY

The gifts that Paul refers to in God's Word are due to the grace of God, and their source is the Holy Spirit. However, there are natural talents all of us have which are gifts of our physical bodies; but the believer has supernatural gifts given to him at the time of salvation. Therefore, it can be defined as "a God-given ability for service." They are given for the common good of the body of Christ.

LESSON 29

The Gifts of the Spirit   Part III

Now there are varieties of gifts, but the same spirit (1 Cor. 12:4).

But one and the same Spirit works all these things, distributing to each one individually just as He wills (1 Cor. 12:11).

AIM: To review the doctrine (teaching) on the gifts of the Spirit and how it relates to the Christian

INTRODUCTION: In review, Jesus was concerned enough with His Church, starting with all of the needed abilities and equipment. He knew that there would be conflict with Satan and his demons. Eph. 4:8 _____

_____

_____,

says that Jesus Himself "gave gifts to men." Through His Spirit the gifts are given, as well as the power of enablement to use them. God knew what was needed in order to fight Satan, and God has provided it. Without the supernatural gifts, the church would be just another social service organization trying to put a bandage on a severed limb.

LESSON:

I. THE GIFT OF THE SPIRIT AND GIFTS OF THE SPIRIT

In our lessons, we will discover that there is a difference between the *gift* of the Holy Spirit and the *gifts* of the Spirit. The *gift* of the Spirit was given to believers as an answer to Jesus'

116

prayer and the promise of the Father. The *gifts* of the Spirit are given by the Spirit for enabling believers to accomplish His will.

At Pentecost, the *gift* of the Spirit was given to the disciples in the upper room. Later, in another incident, the same *gift* of the Spirit was given to some Gentiles. Look up Acts 2:38:

_____

_____

_____.

Also look up Acts 10:44 _____

_____.

The gift of the Spirit is for every believer, but the *gifts* of the Spirit are selectively given to every believer by the same Spirit. Look at 1 Corinthians 12:11 _____

_____

_____.

According to John 14:16 _____

_____,

the *gift* of the Spirit is eternal and will always be, but the *gifts* of the Spirit can fall into disuse and become weak as a muscle that has atrophied through lack of exercise.

The *gift* of the Spirit awaits our appropriating His power in our lives. He does not control where He is not in control. Without His guiding influence in the believer's life, there is no effectiveness in living for Christ. However, the *gifts* of the Spirit are given so the body can be edified, and if a believer chooses not to use his/her gift for the kingdom, then his/her gift is not taken from them. They can develop it both to godly and ungodly uses. We will discuss in the next few lessons more detail concerning the gifts of the Spirit.

II. THE GIFTS OF THE SPIRIT AND THE FRUIT OF THE SPIRIT

Along with a difference between the *gift* of the Spirit and the *gifts* of the Spirit, there is also a difference between the *gifts* of the Spirit and the *fruit* of the Spirit. There are twenty gifts listed in the New Testament and according to Galatians 5:22-23

_____

_____

_____

_____ ,

there are nine different qualities of fruit that are to be in a believer's life.

There are four main differences between the gifts of the Spirit and the fruit of the Spirit. They are:

A. 1. A gift may be externally given and could remain separate from the person who has received it. Without development and use, it will remain as a separate area of that person's life.

   2. Fruit is not something that is given from without but is produced from within.

B. 1. All of the fruit can be produced in any life.

   2. All of the gifts are not given to every believer; neither can they be produced.

C. 1. Gifts are distributed by the Spirit to the believer who is chosen to receive them.

   2. Fruit is distributed; it is developed from within.

D. 1. Gifts are plural in number.

   2. Fruit is singular in number.

Having gifts is no sign of being spiritually mature, for Paul wrote in 1 Corinthians 1:7 _____

_____ ,

that they had no lack in the *gifts* of the Spirit, yet they did not have evidence of the mature *fruit* of the Spirit. Jesus told a true test of maturity in the Christian life in Matthew 7:16

_____

_____ .

Satan can imitate gifts, but he has no power to imitate the fruit of the Spirit.

III. A MEANING OF SPIRITUAL GIFTS

There are two words in the New Testament that are translated as "gifts." They are *pneumatika* and *charismata*. Another word used is *dorea/doma* found in Ephesians 4. From the original Greek, the word "gifts" in 1 Corinthians 12:1 means "derived or originating from the Spirit." G. Campbell Morgan shares that this word is *spiritualities*.

In 1 Corinthians 12:4, *charismata* means "gifts of grace," according to Vine. They are given regardless of human effort or merit. The two words *pneumatika* and *charismata*, taken together, suggest that the gifts are supernatural in origin and provide unusual power to perform services for the body of Christ. They are different from the natural abilities of man.

"The gifts of the Spirit may be classified as:

A. Gifts which qualify their possessors for the ministry of the word: apostleship, prophecy, teaching, shepherding, evangelism, knowledge and wisdom, kinds of tongues, interpretation of tongues, discerning of spirits. Rom. 12:6-8; 1 Cor. 12:4-11,28-30; Eph. 4:7-12.

B. Gifts which equip their possessors to render services of a practical nature: miracles, healing, administration, ruling, helps."[1]

No believer has all the gifts, yet all have a gift. The Word says that, "The manifestation of the Spirit is given to every man." This does not suggest that all believers are using their gift(s) that they have been given. Some believers do not know what their gift is, yet it is clear from God's Word that each person in Christ has at least one of the gifts of the Spirit.

Paul uses the imagery of a human body in describing the body of Christ and His members. Each part of the body is necessary in order that the whole body can function properly. It is the same in the body of Christ. Each member has his/her respective role and function that is crucial to the effective operation of the church. When one person is not functioning as designed, then the whole body suffers.

IV. SUMMARY

Can a believer ever lose his/her gift(s)? This proves to be a problem for some believers when they see other believers, who are supposed to be mature spiritually, living carnal lives and yet experiencing blessings. There are certain serious problems when certain "great" preachers hold positions of authority, and yet their lives are less than admirable as examples. They even seem to have more success than those who are sincere and godly. Why is this so?

J. Oswald Sanders states in his book, *The Holy Spirit and His Gifts,* "If spiritual gifts were the outcome of the filling (control) of the Holy Spirit, or if they were dependent on the continuance of this experience, they would automatically disappear when tolerated sin grieved the Holy Spirit. It would seem, however, that they are given at conversion, and their continued exercise is not dependent on a high plane of Christian living, as for example in the case of the highly-gifted but corrupt and divided Corinthian Church. Samson continued to perform mighty feats for a long time after he was out of touch with God.

"Without dogmatism it is suggested that for this reason the continued possession of spiritual gifts is no criterion of the spiritual state of the possessor, whether it be oneself or another. It would seem that while sin inevitably affects the production of the fruit of the Spirit, it does not affect the gifts to the same degree."[2] Rom. 11:29 _____

_____

_____

_____

_____.

LESSON 30

The Gifts of the Spirit Part IV

Apostles

And He gave some as apostles, and prophets, and some as evangelists, and some as pastors, and teachers, for the equipping of the saints for the work of service, to the building up of the Body of Christ (Eph. 4:11-12).

AIM: To discover the gift of *apostleship* and how it relates to the believer

INTRODUCTION: From the viewpoint of Paul, there was a difference between gifts given to men and men given to the body of believers. In Ephesians he lists five different ministries for the edifying of believers. In 1 Corinthians and Romans, he lists the gifts themselves.

Being an apostle was one of the highest orders of gifts given by the Spirit. Next to Christ, his level of importance was necessary for the birth of the church since Christ had returned to heaven. We will discuss the different aspects of an apostle's ministry in the early church.

LESSON:

I. APOSTLES

The word *apostles* comes from the Greek word *apostolos,* which means a messenger, one sent forth with orders to complete. There are four qualifications to be an apostle. They are:

A. *"They must have seen Jesus.*

B. *They must have been a witness of the resurrection.*

C. *They must have been called by Christ or the Holy Spirit.*

D. *They must have the miraculous powers as credentials of their office.*"[1]

With these qualifications, it is easy to see that this was a temporary gift. They were limited only to the original apostles at the birth of the church. There are no successors to this group.

John R. W. Stott says, "The word 'apostle' is probably used in three senses in the New Testament . . .

(1) In the general sense that all of are sent into the world by Christ and thus share in the apostolic mission of the church, John 17:18 _____

_____

John 20:31 _____

_____,

all of us are in the broadest term 'apostles' . . .

(2) The word is used at least twice to describe 'apostles of the churches,' (2 Cor. 8:23 _____

_____;

Phil. 2:28 _____

_____);

messengers sent on particular errands from one church to another. In this sense the word might be applied to missionaries and other Christians sent on special missions . . .

(3) The gift of 'apostleship' which is thus given precedence must refer, therefore, to that small and special group of men who were 'apostles of Christ,' consisting of the Twelve (Luke 6:12-13 _____

_____

_____),

together with Paul (e.g. Gal. 1:1 _____

_____

_____),

. . . They were unique in being eyewitnesses of the historic Jesus, especially of the risen Lord . . . In this primary sense, therefore, in which they appear in the lists, they have no successors, in the very nature of the case, although there are no doubt 'apostles' today in the secondary sense of 'missionaries.'"[1]

II. SUMMARY

According to J. C. Lambert, "the apostolate was not a limited circle of officials holding a well-defined position of authority in the church, but a large class of men who discharged one—and that the highest—of the functions of the prophetic ministry."

In the New Testament, the word was used in a twofold manner. First, it was used in a limited sense as the official name of Christ's twelve personally selected disciples, who were present after the resurrection and helped to lay a foundation for the church. Secondly, it was used in a broader sense of designating missionaries who were called by the Spirit and sent out by the local church, such as Barnabas in Acts 13:3 _____

_____

_____.

The apostles' authority was not limited to the Church in Jerusalem but covered the entire body of believers.

LESSON 31

The Gifts of the Spirit   Part V

Prophets

And He gave some as apostles, and prophets, and some as evangelists, and some as evangelists, and some as pastors and teachers, for the equipping of the saints for the work of service, to the building up of the Body of Christ (Eph. 4:11-12).

AIM: To discover the gift of *prophets* and how it relates to the believer

INTRODUCTION: The prophet in the New Testament era ministered to the church as a whole and not to a specific local body of believers. His function was as a proclaimer of the truth rather than a predictor of the future. He was a forth-teller and not a fore-teller, though he was able at times to see future events, as in the case of Agabus in Acts 11:27-28 _____

_____

_____

_____

_____.

LESSON:

I. PROPHETS

The English word *prophecy* comes from the Greek word *propheto*, meaning "to publicly expound or to foretell." In biblical times, the gift of prophecy was twofold:

A. Proclaiming the Word from God to man through a prophet. It was a supernatural gift from God in order to share His Word to men.

In order for people to discern true prophets from the false prophets, the Spirit gave the gift of discerning of spirits to other believers to counteract the counterfeit activity of Satan.

The fact that prophets spoke by revelation from God encouraged to some extent the existence of false prophets. They occurred not only in the New Testament but also in the Old Testament. Paul admonished believers not to despise prophesying, but they were also told to test all things. Look up 1 Corinthians 14:3 and record your observations concerning prophesying. _____

_____

_____

_____

B. The second aspect of being a prophet was the ability to edify, instruct, console, and exhort believers in local churches. The prophet was usually a traveling minister, called today an "itinerant" preacher. He had priority over the local pastor. As the church matured, the gift of prophecy was later exercised by local preachers who proclaimed the Word of God to edify the believers under their care.

The gift of prophecy, in the sense of foretelling, no longer exists to the point that it did during New Testament times. There is no longer any "new truth" from God. What He has said is it, and there is nothing to be added. Dr. Merrill C. Tenney states that prophecy *"is the extended sense of presenting God's people truths received, not by direct revelation, but from careful study of the completed and infallible Word of God."*

II. SUMMARY

The unfailing mark of prophecy is that God's voice is heard because it is inspired by Him. The emphasis, however, is not on predicting the future but on telling what He has said. The prophet spoke to *edify, exhort,* and *comfort.* If prophecy is from God, it will not conflict with His written Word. It was a gift that

Paul encouraged believers to "covet." Look up the following verses concerning prophecy and record your observations.
1 Cor. 14:1,15,22,29,31,37 _____

_____

_____

_____

_____

_____

_____

LESSON 32

The Gifts of the Spirit   Part VI

Evangelists

And He gave some as apostles, and prophets, and some as evange-lists, and some as pastors and teachers, for the equipping of the saints for the work of service, to the building up of the Body of Christ (Eph. 4:11-12).

AIM: To discover the gift of an *evangelist* and how it relates to the believer

INTRODUCTION: An evangelist was a man of God who an-nounced the good news of the kingdom. He possessed the spe-cial gift of proclaiming the gospel message so well that many people came to know Christ through his ministry. He started churches and then built up pastors and teachers. Like the prophet, he was a traveling preacher among the unbelievers. He had neither the prestige nor prominence of an apostle or a prophet.

LESSON:

I. EVANGELIST

The word *evangelist* comes from the Greek word *euange-listes*, which means a messenger of good or one who an-nounces some good news. Leighton Ford in his book *Good News Is for Sharing*, states that *"the word translated evangelist occurs only three times in the New Testament:*

(1) Luke called Philip an evangelist (Acts 21:8);

(2) Paul said God gave evangelists to the churches (Eph. 4:11);

*(3) He also urged Timothy to 'do the work of an evangelist'
(2 Tim. 4:5)."*

The gift of evangelism was the ability to share the gospel effectively. The function of the evangelist was similar to the pioneering missionary that we have today. He was not limited just to preaching salvation, but he also established new believers and put them into churches.

II. AN EVANGELIST'S MESSAGE

The message of an evangelist centers around the content of the gospel, for without this key to the kingdom, he was merely another man preaching some "new doctrine." He is primarily a messenger and a deliverer of the good news. An evangelist could both teach and pastor people, but his priority was to proclaim the death, burial, and resurrection of Christ, His coming again, and the need for repentance and belief from all.

He was a special proclaimer of the good news that God was in Christ reconciling the world to Himself.

III. TRUE EVANGELISM

Evangelism can be anything that speaks of sharing a message. However, true evangelism shares the only true message that can change men's hearts. If it is shared with the intellect of a person it may produce some or no emotions. Therefore, it must speak to the will of a person as well.

Not only are there professional evangelists like Billy Graham, who spend their entire lives sharing the gospel, but the gift is sometimes given to the layperson as well. A biblical example is Philip, who was the only person called an evangelist, and he was a deacon. If a believer does not have the gift of evangelism, *he/she is still responsible to do the work of an evangelist.*

IV. METHODS AND MINISTRY OF AN EVANGELIST

Methods of evangelism change with the times, but the message stays the same. It must remain true to the Word in order for people to come to know Christ as Savior. It is, however, not the evangelist who brings conviction of sin, righteousness, or judgment, but the Holy Spirit. Only the Spirit can convert people to Christ. It is the evangelist who is the instrument whom God uses to bring persons to Himself on a large scale.

V. SUMMARY

All of us are not called to be a Billy Graham or Dwight L. Moody, but we are called to do the work of an evangelist like Timothy. 2 Tim. 2:5 _____

_____.

An evangelist, as well as all believers, must have his message, ministry, and life-style founded upon a Spirit-filled, fruit-producing life. Jesus promised in Mark 1:17 _____

_____

_____.

Jesus Himself provides strength through the Spirit to do this arduous work. We all are to do the work of an evangelist, whether or not we go into full-time evangelism. We have no option from God's Word. It is a command found in Matthew that is recorded right from the lips of Christ Himself, right after His resurrection. Write down Matthew 28:19-20 and list your responsibilities concerning doing the work of an evangelist.

_____

_____

_____

_____

_____

LESSON 33

The Gifts of the Spirit   Part VII

Pastors

And He gave some as apostles, and prophets, and some as evangelists, and some as pastors and teachers, for the equipping of the saints for the work of service, to the building up of the Body of Christ (Eph. 4:11-12).

AIM: To discover the gift of a *pastor* and how it relates to the believer

INTRODUCTION: The word pastor does not appear too often in our translations from the original languages. However, it is used both in the Old and New testaments. In the Old Testament, it is translated *shepherd*. That is the underlying meaning of the word pastor. The New Testament used the word "pastor" only once as it relates to being a "shepherd." It is located in Ephesians 4:11 _____

_____,

and is used in connection with the word teacher. There are other references to the word for pastor, but they are not the root word for pastor.

The word pastor is a term used today by the church to refer to ordained ministers. In its original meaning, the use is consistent with what Jesus said about being a Shepherd. Those men who are called to pastor are only "undershepherds" of the local church.

LESSON:

I. THE MEANING OF PASTOR

The word pastor comes from the Greek root word *poimen*

meaning "to protect," hence "shepherd." Jesus used a verb form of this word when He told Peter, "Feed My sheep," in John 21:16 _____

_____

_____.

The word used in most translations is "feed," which actually means to "shepherd."

Peter also employed a verb form in 1 Peter 5:2 when he said

_____

_____

_____.

Paul also used it in Acts 20:28 when he wrote _____

_____

_____.

In Ephesians 4:11-12, Paul puts the two gifts of *pastors* and *teachers* together because they were often found together. When we evaluate it, the *shepherd* or *pastor* has the responsibility of feeding the flock. Therefore, he must also have the ability to be a *teacher* in order to feed.

II. THE ROLE OF A PASTOR

A pastor's role is threefold:
1. To lead his people according to God's Word;
2. To feed and care for them according to God's Word; and
3. To protect them from the various influences that can prove harmful to the flock.

To pastor is an exacting ministry which makes heavy demands on one's patience and compassion. The pastor must carry his people along the road to Christian maturity by feeding them with God's truth.

III. SUMMARY

The gift of pastoring has to do with *leading, providing for,* and *caring for* the flock that is under his authority. The shepherd needs to be equipped in order to equip his flock. This also in-cludes the ability to teach in order to provide the proper care.

Being a pastor is quite different from being an organizer, pro-moter, or social leader. One must be willing to give himself to the preaching of the Word and prayer. In order to do this he must stay close to the Source through prayer and study, which require time. Acts 6:2-4 _____

_____

_____

_____

_____

_____

_____

_____.

LESSON 34

The Gifts of the Spirit   Part VIII

Teachers

And He gave some as apostles, and prophets, and some as evangelists, and some as pastors and *teachers,* for the equipping of the
saints for the work of service, to the building up of the Body of Christ
(Eph. 4:11-12).

AIM: To discover the gift of a *teacher* and how it relates to the believer

INTRODUCTION: *Teaching* is one of the prominent gifts to the local
church. The teacher's function was to interpret God's Word to
and for his congregation. From Scripture, teaching was a supernatural ability to explain and apply the truths of God's Word.
The teaching was based solely upon a thorough study of the
Word, mixed with the leading of the Holy Spirit. The teacher
taught from God's Word, and therefore his gift was different
from that of a prophet, who received his message directly from
God.

LESSON:

I. THE MEANING AND GOAL OF A TEACHER

The word *teacher* comes from the Greek word *didaskalos,*
which means "instructor." In Ephesians 4:11, Paul wrote that

_____

_____

_____.

The reasoning is that when the gospel is preached, the results are converts who immediately need to be taught. Jesus commanded in Matthew 28:19-20 that _____

_____

_____.

This command to make disciples is followed by the command to "teach."

Teaching is simply a Spirit-given ability to invest into the lives of believers a knowledge of God's Word and the applications to daily living that knowledge can provide. Its goal is that of Romans 8:29 _____

_____.

conformity to Christ.

II. THE FUNCTIONS OF A TEACHER

"William Barclay stated that the teacher had a dual function. In the absence of a written record, they:

1. Were reservoirs of the gospel story for the early Church; and

2. Had to explain the great doctrines (teachings) of the faith. Most of the new believers came direct from heathenism, and were totally ignorant of Christianity and Christ."[1] For them the teacher was a necessity in order for them to grow.

III. SUMMARY

"Teaching is the supernatural ability to explain, in harmony and in detail, God's revelation and it is especially operational in the grounding of new Christians. Its main purpose is to direct the understanding concerning things of a spiritual nature. This New Testament gift was given to explain truths that had already been projected to the church by the apostles and the prophets. Every Christian should know basic truths concerning the faith, but some have the God-given ability to impart these truths to others in a clear manner.

"Today, the gift of teaching has solely to do with 2 Timothy
2:15 _____

_____

_____.

The Scripture is the final revelation from God to men. Everything we need to know about God, Christ, the Holy Spirit, and
about spiritual truth is recorded for us in the Canon. The gift of
teaching is the supernatural ability to 'dig out the milk and the
meat of the Word' and 'feed it to the flock.'"[2]

LESSON 35

Further Gifts of the Spirit   Part IX

For to one is given the word of wisdom through the Spirit, and to another the word of knowledge according to the same Spirit; to another faith by the same Spirit, . . . helps, administrations (1 Cor. 12:8,9a,28b).

AIM: To discover in general other gifts of the Spirit that are listed in the Word of God and find out how they are related to the believer

INTRODUCTION: God gives gifts to every believer at the moment of salvation, but He never gives all of His gifts to any one person. If a person did have all of them, there would not enough time in this life to use all of them.

It is obvious from our previous studies in this manual, that some gifts, like those listed in Ephesians 4:11, _____

_____

_____

_____,

carry with them greater prominence and responsibility. These gifts are usually given to people who will be leading others. There are, however, several more gifts that are not as prominent as the gifts we have already studied. They are less prominent because we do not always see them in action. This does not make them less important, because all of the gifts of the Spirit are vital for the edification of the body of Christ. Let's look at some of the other gifts mentioned in 1 Corinthians 12 and see how they fit together.

LESSON:
I. DEFINITIONS

Look up and record a brief definition of the following gifts as found in a Bible or theological dictionary:

A. Knowledge _____

_____

_____

B. Wisdom _____

_____

_____

C. Faith _____

_____

_____

D. Discernment of Spirits _____

_____

_____

E. Helps _____

_____

_____

F. Government (Administration) _____

_____

_____

II. DIFFERENCE BETWEEN GIFTS AND GRACE

It is important for believers to understand that there is a difference between the gifts of the Spirit and the grace that God gives to help us live the Christian life. Below is a list of spiritual gifts which include the aspect of grace for believers. Write in your own words why you think all of them are necessary to help us live for Christ.

A. Wisdom (Jas. 1:5) _____

_____

_____

_____

B. Knowledge (Eph. 1:17-19) _____

_____

_____

_____

C. Faith (Heb. 11:6) _____

_____

_____

_____

D. Discernment (Heb. 5:14) _____

_____

_____

_____

E. Helps (Gal. 6:10, 5:13) _____

_____

_____

_____

III. BIBLICAL EXAMPLES OF THE USE OF SPIRITUAL GIFTS

There are numerous examples of the use of spiritual gifts by biblical characters. Observing these cases helps us to understand their necessity and operation. Look up the following Scriptures and explain why a gift was necessary and if one or more gifts were used.

A. Peter's gift of discernment (Acts 5:1-10, 8:9-25) _____

_____

_____

_____

B. Peter's gift of knowledge, knowing just what to say (Acts 4:8-13) _____

_____

_____

_____

C. Peter's gift of faith (Acts 3:1-10) _____

_____

_____

_____

D. Paul's gift of faith (Acts 27:13-25) _____

_____

_____

_____

E. Paul's gift of wisdom (Acts 27:27-37) _____

_____

_____

_____

IV. SUMMARY

Along with receiving the gifts of the Spirit, every believer receives the responsibility and an accountability in using his/her gift(s). If we mishandle our gifts we are accountable to God first, and then to the believers among whom the gifts are exercised. Second Corinthians 5:10-15 gives us insight that an evaluation time will come at the end of our sojourn here. As you read this passage, what are the possible results of this final evaluation?

_____

_____

_____

_____

_____

What is the evaluation of your life and work for the Lord as of today? _____

_____

_____

_____

_____

LESSON 36

Further Gifts of the Spirit   Part X

Word of Wisdom, Word of Knowledge

For to one is given the word of wisdom through the Spirit, and to another the word of knowledge according to the same spirit; to another faith by the same spirit; . . . helps, administrations (1 Cor. 12:8,9a,28b).

AIM: To discover specifically the gifts of the *word of wisdom* and the *word of knowledge* and how they relate to the believer

INTRODUCTION: In 1 Corinthians 12:4, Paul says: "Now there are varieties of gifts, but the same spirit." What Paul means by this is that there is *only one* Holy Spirit, and He has the ability to give many different kinds of gifts. Whatever we discuss in this lesson is based upon the assumption that gifts are supernatural in origin and come from the Spirit. The believer cannot manufacture these gifts, yet some people have the ability to imitate some of the gifts. We called it a counterfeit gift. As it relates to understanding clearly the implications of the gifts of the Spirit, we are to study God's Word and apply it to our own level of maturity in Christ.

The Holy Spirit does give to some people a unique degree of wisdom, knowledge, and faith. Because some may have these gifts and others do not, does not mean that other believers are any less complete in Christ. Generally speaking, these gifts are often enhanced forms of ordinary abilities that all believers have. We will be discussing the gifts of *wisdom* and *knowledge* in this lesson.

LESSON:

I. DEFINITION

Dr. Merrill C. Tenney defines the word of wisdom as *"the ability to make correct decisions on the basis of one's knowledge."* Accepting this definition of this gift leads us to the word of knowledge, which concerns familiarity with spiritual insights. A word of wisdom is a result of direct insight into spiritual truths, based not only upon study of the Word, but also from a deep fellowship with God. *"Clement of Alexandria defined wisdom as 'the knowledge of things human and divine, and of their causes.'"*[1] The believers who possess this gift are well worth hearing and heeding because God does not give gifts merely for the sake of giving them. They are to edify other believers in the church.

The *word of knowledge* is more practical in the sense that it applies the *word of wisdom* to daily living. Though some believers possess more than one gift, these two gifts of wisdom and knowledge are not necessarily given to the same person. Even numerous knowledgeable believers lack wisdom.

II. SUMMARY

There are many believers with special information about God and His Word, but who do not know how to apply it on a daily basis. Therefore, the gifts of wisdom and knowledge need to work together.

In Mark 13:11 _____

_____,

Jesus shares insight where a believer may need the use of both gifts. More often than not, the disciples of Christ had to defend themselves in various situations. For example, Paul probably made his defense before Caesar himself. The knowledge that comes from the gift of knowledge is the result of a serious study of His Word. To apply what we have learned from the Word involves more than study, and we need the help of the Holy

Spirit to make the difference. Wisdom is the gift that shows us how to use the knowledge we have gained.

Through our fellowship with God and a sincere study of the Word, we will gain a deeper understanding of living life than what the world proclaims. Believers who have these gifts to an enhanced degree should consider that they have the gift of wisdom or knowledge.

LESSON 37

Further Gifts of the Spirit   Part XI

Faith

To another faith by the same spirit . . . (1 Cor. 12:9a).

AIM: To discover specifically the gift of *faith* and how it relates to the believer

INTRODUCTION: In this lesson, we are not focusing on saving faith. Though it is a gift from God, it is not the gift as outlined in 1 Corinthians 12:9a. The gift of faith is a wonder-working faith that can move mountains. 1 Cor. 13:2 _____

_____

_____.

The context of the verse above supports this view. It is a specific gift of extraordinary faith that is given in order for the believer who possesses it to carry out a special ministry of the Lord. George Müller, for example, had this gift to a large degree, but many people have possessed and exercised this gift—the faith that can turn visions into reality.

LESSON:

I. DEFINITION

The word *faith* comes from a Greek word meaning faithfulness, unwavering or immovable. 1 Cor. 12:9a _____

_____.

In this passage, Paul assumes the existence of saving faith. The Scripture says in Ephesians 2:8 _____

_____

_____.

We are also told in 2 Corinthians 5:7 _____

_____

_____.

With all of this, however, faith, in 1 Corinthians 12, is a special gift that the Holy Spirit gives as He wills.

II. DIFFERENCE BETWEEN FAITH AND THE GIFT OF FAITH

There is a big difference between saving faith and the gift of faith. Saving faith means that God will do what He has promised to do in His Word to bring us into a relationship with Him. After this point, our faith is no longer saving faith but an experiential faith which allows us to believe that God will do whatever He has promised to do in His Word. All believers have this experiential faith. Therefore, as Hebrews 11:6 says _____

_____,

and if we do not have faith in Him or His Word, then we sin. But there are visions and dreams we have where there are no specific promises from His Word. As a result we pray and declare "if it be Thy will," but the Holy Spirit gives us the gift of faith to believe that He will help bring things to pass if we are obedient to His leading. If we do not have this gift, it is not a sin.

III. AN EXAMPLE OF THE EXERCISE OF THE GIFT OF FAITH

"There is a classic example of the gift of faith in the life of George Müller of Bristol, England, who cared for thousands of orphans over a period of many years. Müller refused to ask anyone for a single penny, but he prayed the money in. This gift of faith is described by Jesus when He said in Matthew 17:20

_____

_____."1

LESSONS ON THE HOLY SPIRIT

IV. SUMMARY

The gift of faith in this context means the supernatural ability to believe God's power to supply specific needs. Every believer has a measure of experiential faith in that one has to have faith in order to be saved, but not every believer has the gift of faith. NOT everyone has an outstanding measure of faith. Do not be confused! Gifts are NOT the gauge of your spiritual maturity. All God's children should believe their Father, but there are some differences between faith and the gift of faith. Otherwise, it would not be listed as a separate gift.

LESSON 38

Further Gifts of the Spirit   Part XII

Discernment of Spirits

And to another the distinguishing of spirits . . . (1 Cor. 12:10).

AIM: To discover specifically the gift of *discernment of spirits* and how it relates to the believer

INTRODUCTION: This gift is a gift on gifts. It is the ability to discern or distinguish between true and false spirits and gifts. In 1 John 4:6 we read _____

_____,

which tells us that we are able to discern the spirit of truth from the spirit of error. The reason for this gift in New Testament times was because there was no written New Testament and therefore, when someone claimed to be of Christ, there was nothing to judge whether they were true to His teachings or not. This gift enabled the New Testament church to keep out false teachings, demonic manifestations, and psychic phenomena. Let's look a little more closely at this unique gift on gifts.

LESSON:

I. DEFINITION

The word for *discernment* in 1 Corinthians 12:10 comes from the Greek root word *diakrisis* which means to "judge closely, examine as under a microscope, consider all the information, to see through to the bottom line." The *New American Standard Bible* translates it as "the distinguishing of spirits." It was used by the possessor to evaluate whether a spirit or gift was from God or from some spirit other than the Holy Spirit.

147

II. THE NEED FOR DISCERNMENT

Paul states in 2 Corinthians 11:14-15 _____

_____

_____

_____ .

With this in mind, the fact of the appearance of many false prophets and deceivers should be no surprise to believers. The Bible predicts that they will increase in activity at the end of the age. In the New Testament Church, this gift guarded the church from inadvertently accepting anything that claimed to have come from God. A. T. Robertson says, "It was given to tell whether the gifts were really of the Holy Spirit and supernatural . . . or . . . merely natural or even diabolical!"

III. TEST THE SPIRITS

We are to test the spirits and gifts that are existing today. What is the standard by which we must test these spirits? The Word of God is the ruler by which we measure. Even today, God still gives some believers the ability to discern truth. In 1 Corinthians 12:10 we read _____

_____ .

Thus the gift of discernment allowed Peter to sift through the hypocrisy of Ananias and Sapphira. He also discerned that Simon of Samaria was not concerned about the kingdom but only establishing his own kingdom. Read Acts 8:9ff. In 1 Timothy 4:1 _____

_____ ,

Paul warned believers that "some will fall away from the faith, paying attention to deceitful spirits and doctrines of demons."

Anything that seems to be religious ought to be carefully evaluated by a believer before approval is given as acceptable. This also should include some churches to see if they are sound in their teachings before we become members.

IV. SUMMARY

Always let the Scriptures be your guide for discerning truth and error. Never accept what you hear until you have checked it out in God's word. In certain cases you may need to consult some mature believer whose opinions you trust, asking them for advice concerning spiritual matters in relation to the Word of God.

The gift of discernment allows a believer to tell whether gifts are truly from God or from some other spirit. The admonition from John to "test the spirits" has this as its aim, and it is still necessary today when cults and heresies are prevalent and pervasive.

LESSON 39

Further Gifts of the Spirit   Part XIII

Helps

And God has appointed . . . helps, . . . (1 Cor. 12:28)

AIM: To discover specifically the gift of helps and how it relates to the believer

INTRODUCTION: The gifts of the Spirit are service-oriented toward being used within the body of Christ as aids to development and encouragement, but the *gift of helps* is a particular, specialized gift of service. There are no boundaries that hinder the exercise of this gift, and it has unlimited range in dealing with the sick, widows, poor, orphans, or the old. This gift goes beyond general helpfulness and is a special, God-given ability to help others. For those in the church who do not have one of the speaking gifts, it allows endless possibilities for ministry.

LESSON:

I. DEFINITION

The gift of "helps" mentioned in 1 Corinthians 12:28 comes from the Greek word *antilepsis*, which means to support or assist. Literally it means "to take a burden off of someone else and place it on yourself." The verb above is used by Paul in Acts 20:25 concerning the Ephesian believers. Acts 20:25

_____

_____

_____.

II. EXAMPLE

An example of the use of helps occurs in Acts 6. It may have specific reference to the work of deacons, for in Acts 6:1-3,

_____

_____

_____,

the apostles did not have time to "serve tables." As a result they called the first deacons, servers—for originally the word meant to "wait on tables." They were assigned to wait on tables and to distribute funds to the poor. Because these deacons accepted this responsibility, it made it possible for other lay people to contribute to the kingdom by praying, counseling, administrative functions in the church and other Christian organizations, and also to witness.

Look up the following verses and give your observations concerning the "service" aspect of helping.

1 Tim. 6:2 _____

_____

_____

Rom. 16:3,9 _____

_____

_____

_____

Phil. 2:25-30 _____

_____

_____

_____

III. WHAT DOES HELPS CONSIST OF?

Helps carries with it more than the idea of helping someone through prayer. It includes social services that help the oppressed, which includes those who experience social injustices and the care of the senior citizens, as well as for widows and orphans. Practically, this gift could mean visiting someone in the hospital, writing letters to prisoners, or sharing our resources with those in need. Aiding the leadership is also one of the aspects this gift could manifest, allowing the leadership to use their gifts more freely. Look up 1 Peter 4:11 and record your impressions concerning its implications relating to helps.

_____

_____

_____

_____

IV. SUMMARY

Though this is a specialized gift of the Spirit, it does not negate the responsibilities of other believers to be aware of needs and meet those needs as they see them. Waiting on someone who may have the gift is irresponsible action and should always be avoided. Read the letter to Philemon to discover aspects of Onesimus's gifts of "helps."

LESSON 40

Further Gifts of the Spirit   Part XIV

Administrations or Rulings

And God has appointed . . . administrations, . . . (1 Cor. 12:28).

AIM: To discover specifically the gift of administrations or governments and rulings, and how that gift relates to the believer

INTRODUCTION: "The Scriptures teach that churches must have government; they require leadership, whether professional or non-professional. Christ spent more than half His time with just twelve men, developing them into leaders who would carry on His work after He ascended to heaven. Wherever the apostles went they appointed leaders over the churches they founded. The Scripture says in Acts 14:23: _____

_____.

In 1 Timothy 3:1-7, Paul gives qualifications for 'bishops' (KJV). The word for 'bishop' is thought by many to be equivalent to 'pastor,' carrying the idea of overseer, superintendent, or governor."[1]

LESSON:

I. THE MEANING OF ADMINISTRATION / GOVERNMENT AND RULINGS

The term "governments," which occurs only in 1 Corinthians 12:28, is the word for the "steersman of a ship, who guides it through rocks and shoals to harbor. The word 'rulers' means 'the one standing in front,' or the leader. In any work of God, leadership and a certain amount of administration are necessary, and the Spirit imparts special gifts for this work. It is work that is unspectacular and demanding, and not always appreciated. Nevertheless, it is necessary to the smooth functioning of the work of the kingdom."[2]

It refers to a person who is at the controls of a ship, who charts the course, knows where he is going, and has enough experience and control to keep his ship on course.

Leadership is the ability to see a goal, make plans or steps of action to reach that goal, and then motivate others to join in to reach that goal. It is more than having a position but knowing what to do in that position. A leader realizes that he does not own the "ship" but is just a steward in charge.

II. QUALIFICATIONS OF AN ADMINISTRATOR/RULER

There are several New Testament qualifications that a person with the gift of administration should have. He cannot be a dictator or have an inflated ego that all depends upon him, and he must not be dogmatic. He is, however, to have a spirit of humility, a graciousness in attitude, and to be courteous, kind, and loving. In short, he should have the fruit of the Spirit present in his life. He must be able to be both tough and tender when the need arises.

III. JESUS, THE PERFECT ADMINISTRATOR/RULER

Jesus Himself was the best example of what the gift of administration should be like. Look up the following Scriptures and record your thoughts concerning Jesus' ability to rule.

Mark 10:45 _____

_____

Phil. 2:7 _____

_____

John 13:16 _____

_____

By His example we see that a ruler should be a servant most of all, a helper, or even a slave. What are we exhorted to do in Galatians 5:13? _____

_____

From the original Greek, this is interpreted to be a command and not merely an optional duty, and it has special significance to rulers.

IV. SUMMARY

This gift is vital to the nature and work of the church and is not given to all believers. This gift in relation to the church is the ability to lead a church. All Christians are on the same level as it relates to our position "in Christ," but not all are given places of higher authority.

Do not compare the biblical gift of administration with natural administrative abilities. They are not the same, though the natural abilities could be exercised through the church. However, the gift is *not* a natural ability, but a supernatural ability, and the Scriptures admonish us to give proper heed to the ones who have been given this gift.

LESSON 41

Further Gifts of the Spirit   Part XV

The Sign Gifts
Miracles, Tongues, and Healing

And to another the effecting of miracle, . . . to various kinds of tongues, and to another the interpretation of tongues . . . then the gifts of healings, . . . (1 Cor. 12:10,28).

AIM: To give brief insight into the sign gifts of miracles, tongues, and healing and how they relate to the believer

INTRODUCTION: It is interesting that three of the gifts given by the Spirit for the common good of all have become the source of great controversy and often division. They are often called the "sign gifts" because of their visible manifestations of God's power and include the gifts of healing, miracles, and tongues (1 Cor. 12:8-10 _____

_____

_____

_____).

Signs are excellent for drawing attention and are given to point to Christ. They have often become an end in themselves and are sometimes used to prove a point. Highway signs do not usually mark locations but simply point in their direction. As related to Jesus Christ, signs were given to point persons to Him and let them know that *when they saw a sign* the One greater than the sign was nearby. Jesus rebuked many Jews who were looking for a sign rather than a Savior (Matt. 12:38-39 _____

_____

_____).

156

When He corrected them, He would always point to the greatest sign—His death and resurrection.

LESSON:
I. THE GIFT OF MIRACLES

Miracles represent a supernatural intervention in the natural order of the universe. Often, in the New Testament era, they authenticated the message of the apostles, so they were identified with Jesus Christ, and on some occasions they were not present as with John the Baptist's messengers in John 10:41-42

_____

_____

_____

_____.

Paul states in 2 Corinthians 12:12 that _____

_____

_____.

This gives us an idea that miracles validated an apostle's ministry in the New Testament. Christ Himself performed miracles. Look up the following Scriptures and record your ideas concerning the types of miracles He performed.

Luke 4:36 _____

_____;

Luke 6:17-19 _____

_____;

Mark 1:34 _____

_____;

Luke 9:42-43 _____

_____;

Matt. 8:16 _____

_____.

The apostles also performed miracles. Look up the following

verses and record your thoughts concerning the type of miracles
they performed.

Luke 10:17-19 _____

_____ ;

Rom. 15:19 _____

_____ ;

2 Cor. 12:12 _____

_____ .

II. THE GIFT OF TONGUES

The gift of tongues is one of the most controversial topics today. Though the church at Corinth used this gift both to God's
glory and abused it to God's grief, the same situation is true today. First Corinthians chapter 14 covers the subject adequately
and in Lessons 43—45 of this study manual, we will discuss this
gift in fuller detail.

Like the other gifts of the Spirit, this gift is not referred to as a
mark of spiritual maturity or faith in Christ and is not claimed to
be available to every believer. In comparison with the other
gifts, it has the most strings attached to it because of the dangers
involved in its abuse; and in priority, it is ranked behind prophecy. However, we are commanded by Paul in 1 Corinthians
14:39 _____

_____ .

Judge for yourself if this lends validity to its use today. Whether
or not one has the gift of tongues, he/she has a strong urging
always to act in love (see 1 Corinthians 13:1-3), which will deter
most abuses of any of the gifts.

III. THE GIFT OF HEALING

The gift of healing means the gift of cures. It is most often
misunderstood as to its purpose, method, and range of applica-
tion. Some believe that healing was provided for in the atonement and should be claimed for all who are sick. The Scripture
that is used most often is Isaiah 53:5 _____

_____

_____.

If the purpose of healings were only physical, then many of us who are believers suffer needlessly. And as it relates to Christ Himself, why did He not heal Paul of his affliction? See 2 Corinthians 12:9-10 _____

_____

_____

_____,

and why was Timothy not healed of his ailment (1 Tim. 5:23

_____

_____),

and not given a medicinal prescription by Paul?

In another example (John 9:2-3) Jesus gave an explanation for a man's blindness _____

_____

_____

_____.

He taught that it was God's will to display His works in Him. Above all, the Healer is more important than the healing. If it is accomplished by the gift of healing or of faith, by medicine, or by being taken home to be with the Lord—the glory should always go to the Lord.

IV. ADDITIONAL INVESTIGATION

A. Gifts have a way of revealing something about the Giver and the receiver. From the brief discussion of this lesson on miracles, tongues, and healing, what have you learned concerning the Holy Spirit as the Giver and man as the receiver? What have you learned concerning God's character, message, method, and motives? How are our needs as believers met through these gifts? _____

_____

_____

_____

_____

_____

_____

B. Some people teach that all believers should have certain
   sign gifts. What insights do you gain from 1 Corinthians
   12:29-30, _____

   _____ ,

   about the distribution of gifts? _____

   _____

   _____

   _____

   _____ .

   Look also at 1 Corinthians 12:4-6,11 _____

   _____

   _____

   _____

   _____ .

C. When we study Scriptures relating to miracles, we often
   center in on the event of the miracle and not on the results
   or its effect upon others. Look up the following Scriptures
   and write down the results and those who were affected by
   each sign gift.
   Acts 4:33 _____

   _____

   _____

   _____

   Acts 8:5-7 _____

   _____

   _____

   _____

Acts 13:9-12 _____

_____

_____

_____

Acts 16:16-18 _____

_____

_____

_____

VI. SUMMARY

Perhaps as you compare the gifts of other believers to yours, you may become envious, jealous, or resentful. Or perhaps you may feel the opposite and think of others who do not have your gift(s) to be inferior. If either is the case, and if you have been tempted to be divisive when you discuss spiritual gifts, why not confess this to the Lord, asking Him to help you promote the unity of the Spirit among believers? Pray for the reality of Ephesians 4:1-6 in your life.

LESSON 42

Further Gifts of the Spirit   Part XVI

Miracles

And to another the effecting of miracles . . . (1 Cor. 12:10a).

AIM: To discover specifically the gift of miracles and how it relates to the believer

INTRODUCTION: The word "miracles," found in 1 Corinthians 12:10a, should be translated "powers." This word is often used concerning the miracles that Jesus performed. Mark 5:30

_____

_____

_____.

In the theme verse above, it begins with, "And to another . . . ," which suggests that the gift of miracles was distinctly different from the gift of healing. Examples of the gift of miracles include the death of Ananias and Sapphira, the smiting of Elymas, the exorcising of demons, and the powers that are mentioned in Mark 16:17 _____

_____

_____.

LESSON:

I. DEFINITION

The gift of miracles is evidenced by the supernatural ability to change the laws of nature. It is a display of power or the ability to go beyond the natural for the glory of God and not for the

162

promotion of self. Jesus Himself possessed the ability to perform miracles. He turned water into wine, calmed the seas, and stilled a wind. The apostles also performed miracles. They raised the dead and even brought blindness to those who could see. There are four biblical observations concerning miracles:

1. God's work in creation began with miracles. In creation, we discover that there were numerous displays of signs and wonders (see Genesis 1—2). After the Exodus and before the giving of the Law, miracles, signs, and wonders occurred in the presence of the Israelites. When Jesus began His ministry in Cana of Galilee, it was a miracle of changing water into wine that signaled His ministry's inception. Therefore, as a summation of biblical facts, at every starting point where God instituted or created a new work, a miracle was included to validate it.

2. After God's work was started, the miracles began to diminish. In Hebrews 2:3-4, we find that _____
   _____
   _____
   _____.

   These verses suggest that God used miracles as a witness to confirm His Word that was given by prophets. At the birth of the church, the disciples performed miracles until the church became well-established in the faith. Then there was no need to give signs of wonder and amazement, for the New Testament was formed to help build up the faith of the believers. As we look into the history of the church, the evidence supports that the gift of miracles ceased at the close of the first century.

3. Though the New Testament gift of miracles no longer exists, it does not mean that miracles themselves no longer happen. In Hebrews 1:10-11, the author states, _____
   _____
   _____
   _____,

and tells us that God will continue to exist and remain the same, even though everything else shall perish. This suggests that He never changes. However, even though He does not change, *His methods and people do*. The New Testament gift of miracles does not occur today, yet some miracles do happen. They are not done with the New Testament gift as in that era, but are done by the sovereign will of God and *cannot be claimed with any amount of human effort*. Only He can do true miracles by changing and altering nature for His expressed purposes.

4. Miracles were and are performed to glorify Christ only. The miracles that God performed through His men were to call attention to Christ and not to the man who performed the miracle. They were "signs" that pointed upward toward Christ and not inward or outward toward men. If the gift of miracles exists today, it must operate under at least two principles.

   A. *It must be performed by the altering of nature, like raising the dead, causing the blind to see, the deaf to hear, and all other forms of miracles*. It will not be limited to only one type of miracle, such as healing. The New Testament example of Christ Himself shows that He performed more than one kind of miracle. Even the apostles did more than heal diseases. God is not limited in His power to perform. Neither is He dependent upon us to do so. He can operate independently of our abilities, and oftentimes He does so in order to give us a testimony of His ability.

   B. *The miracle must always point to Christ and never to the performer*. If a person claims to have the gift of miracles and causes others to follow and honor him rather than Christ, then that gift and that person may be suspect as to their motivations. Refer to Acts 8:9-24. Money, prestige, power, and other enticements are generally the goals of such performers.

II. SUMMARY

As we have concluded, a miracle is an event that occurs beyond the power of the physical laws of nature. It is an occurrence that has its source in God's power. In many translations of the Old Testament, the word "miracle" is translated "a wonder" or "a mighty work." New Testament translations use "signs" as in John 2:11 _____

_____

_____;

or "signs and wonders" as in John 4:48 _____

_____

_____;

Acts 5:12 _____

_____

_____;

or "miracles and wonders" as in Acts 15:12 _____

_____

_____

_____.

Look up all the references in your Bible, using a concordance, that refer to "signs," "miracles," and "wonders." Write down your observations about the type of miracles that were performed and whether the person performing the miracle received the glory or whether he gave the glory to God._____

_____

_____

_____

_____

_____

_____

_____

_____

_____

_____

LESSON 43

Further Gifts of the Spirit   Part XVII

They all began to speak with other tongues (Acts 2:4).

And to another the effecting of miracles . . . to another various kinds of tongues . . . (1 Cor. 12:10).

AIM: To discuss in detail the gift of tongues and how it relates to the Christian

INTRODUCTION: The phenomena accompanying the descent of the Spirit on the day of Pentecost bore clear witness to the release of a new spiritual power, the dawning of a new era. The assembled crowds were confounded by the spectacular gift of speaking with other tongues which the Spirit had imparted to the waiting disciples. All were greatly impressed by the fact that every man heard the disciples speak in his own language. "They were all amazed and marveled." (Acts 2:4-7 _____

_____

_____).

LESSON:

I. WHAT EXACTLY WAS THE GIFT GIVEN AT PENTECOST?

Jesus told His disciples to wait in Jerusalem for the "promise of the Father." Luke 24:29 says: _____

_____

_____

_____.

What was this "power" to be given to those disciples who were waiting? It was the Holy Spirit Who had the power that Jesus promised they would receive. The gift of tongues was given not as evidence of receiving the Spirit but evidence to those people who were present in Jerusalem at that precise moment. This evidence was convincing because the crowd marveled and was amazed at hearing in their own language "the mighty works of God."

These were not vagabonds traveling through but they were "devout men, from every nation under heaven." God in His sovereignty chose exactly who He wanted to be there to hear and see what was taking place. Their conversion to Christ meant that the gospel would be taken to every nation, since every nation was represented in the crowd. The Great Commission was given, and God Himself provided the avenue by which it could be carried out. The gift of tongues was a vehicle through which the gospel could receive an audience. On the day of Pentecost, the vehicle, the audience, and the message came together, and three thousand souls came into the kingdom.

"The gift of tongues, like the sound as of wind, and tongues as of fire, was incidental. The two things (power of enablement, gift of tongues) are distinct and separable. The evidence of the power of enablement of the Spirit was effectiveness and extensiveness in witness. Acts 1:8 _____

_____

_____.

It is true the filling of the Spirit was accompanied by speaking with tongues, but this was neither the gift itself, nor its most significant evidence."[1]

II. DEFINITION OF TONGUES

The Greek word for tongue is *glossa*. It means tongue,

speech, talk, language. It is used interchangeably in Acts 2:1-12 with the Greek word *dialectos*. *Dialectos* means the peculiar language of a nation, speech, language, and jargon. The gift was the ability through the Spirit to speak in a language that was not familiar or not known to the speaker. It was a known language to some of the hearers but was totally unknown to the speaker. Acts 2:1-12 _____

_____

_____

_____

_____

_____.

III. IS IT *OTHER* TONGUES OR *UNKNOWN* TONGUES?

Using Scripture as our guide, are the "other tongues" of Acts 2 and the "unknown tongues" of 1 Corinthians 14 the same? From the original text in the Greek, the word "unknown" is not present in 1 Corinthians 14. It should be read simply "tongues." In Acts 2:4, _____

_____,

"other tongues" occurs. As a matter of recognition, in Acts 10:46 and Acts 19:6, it is translated "with tongues."

E. H. Plumpter says that "apart from the day of Pentecost, the tongues were not 'the power of speaking in a language which had not been learned in the common way of learning, but the ecstatic utterance of rapturous devotion.'"[2]

There are some similarities. However, there are some strong differences between the speaking in tongues at Pentecost and the speaking in tongues at Corinth. Here are some:

1. "At Pentecost all spoke in tongues. Acts 2:4 _____

_____

_____.

This was not true of the believers at Corinth. 1 Cor. 12:30

_____

_____.

2. At Pentecost the tongues were understood by all. Acts 2:6

_____

_____.

At Corinth they were understood by none. 1 Cor. 14:2

_____

_____.

3. At Pentecost they spoke to men. Acts 2:6 _____

_____

_____.

At Corinth they spoke to God. 1 Cor. 14:2,9 _____

_____

_____

_____.

4. At Pentecost no interpreter was necessary. Acts 2:6 _____

_____

_____.

At Corinth tongue-speaking was forbidden if no interpreter
was present. 1 Cor. 14:23,28 _____

_____

_____

_____.

5. At Pentecost tongues were a sign to the Jews. Acts 11:15

_____

_____

_____.

At Corinth it was a sign to unbelievers. 1 Cor. 14:22 ____

_____.

6. At Pentecost strangers were filled with awe and marveled.
Acts 2:7-8 _____

_____

_____.

At Corinth, Paul warned that strangers would say that they were mad. 1 Cor. 14:23 _____

_____

_____.

7. At Pentecost there was perfect harmony. Acts 2:1 _____

_____

_____.

At Corinth there was confusion."[3] 1 Cor. 14:33 _____

_____

_____.

From these differences we find there is not enough similarity to formulate a doctrine or teaching. If the two occurrences are not the same experience, then what are they?

In Acts 2, the experience of "other tongues" was languages that were not familiar to the disciples. The Spirit gave them the ability to speak other intelligible languages that were not noise. The evidence points to the fact that the crowd understood what the disciples were saying. As a contrast, the speaking in tongues of 1 Corinthians 14 was not necessarily understood by the hearers, except through the gift of interpretation. One is understood without the aid of an interpreter, and the other could only be understood with the aid of an interpreter.

IV. ASSESSING THE GIFT OF TONGUES

It is without question that the gift of tongues had significant value when it was given by the Spirit. It was indeed necessary for the growth of the church. Assessing the fact that the Spirit gave this gift at the birth of the Church means that He had use for it and the gift of interpretation of tongues. People are still amazed and interested in the exercise of this gift, as was the crowd on Pentecost Sunday. Paul wrote in 1 Corinthians 14:4

_____

_____ ,

that the speaker "edifieth himself," even though prophecy does more to edify the church. Those who experience speaking in tongues state that there is a new liberty in worship, a sense of freedom and nearness to the Lord. This may be true, but it is also true that the same experiences of freedom in prayer, liberty in worship, etc., are experienced by others through the Spirit's working without speaking in tongues.

Others suggest that the experience of speaking in tongues gives a sense of an objective indication that God is working in that person's life. The intervention of the Spirit using our ability to speak does give an awareness of a supernatural sign. However, Jesus reminded us that an evil and adulterous generation seeks after signs. Seeking signs is a definite mark of spiritual immaturity, and neither Jesus nor Paul encouraged such to build faith. 2 Corinthians 5:7 _____

_____ ,

states that we are to walk by a higher order of faith and not by our senses. If you want to know whether the Spirit is working in your life it is not by the exercising of the gift of tongues, but "by their fruits" and not "by their gifts" ye shall know them.

V. SUMMARY

Paul's teaching on this subject, as contained in 1 Corinthians 14:20-28, can be summarized with the following statements.

1. The gift of tongues was directly related to the Jews. Verse 21

_____

_____ .

This verse is from the book of Isaiah and referred to the Jewish people.

2. The gift of tongues were given for the sole purpose of being a sign to unbelievers. Verse 22 _____

_____

_____.

3. The gift of tongues was to be used for public use and not for private use. It can be used privately but only in the context of the church. Verse 28 _____

_____

_____.

4. The gift of tongues should be controlled by the speaker. Verse 27 _____

_____.

LESSON 44

Further Gifts of the Spirit   Part XVIII

Tongues—2

They all began to speak with other tongues . . . (Acts 2:4).

And to another the effecting of miracles . . . to another various kinds of tongues . . . (1 Cor. 12:10).

AIM: To discuss in detail the gift of tongues and how it relates to the believer

INTRODUCTION: Leon Morris says: "The Corinthians had apparently used the gifts as a means of creating division. They regarded the possession of such gifts as a matter of pride, and set up one against another on the basis of the possession or otherwise of this gift or that. Paul insists that this is the wrong attitude. Though he recognizes that there is diversity in the endowments conferred by the Spirit, yet it is the same Spirit. The Spirit does not fight against Himself. The gifts He gives to one are to set forward the same Divine purpose as the different gifts He gives to another."[1]

LESSON:

I. THE LIMITS TO USEFULNESS

In 1 Corinthians 14, Paul urged the use of tongues but with certain restraints. The reason for this is that he knew and shared with the church in Corinth that there were limits to the value of speaking in tongues. Singling out this gift, Paul issued a restraint because of the nature of tongues-speaking. It can cause a believer to be preoccupied with him/herself, thinking that this gift brings significance and importance above the other gifts of the Spirit. Serving the church can take the back seat to the performance of the gift. In 1 Corinthians 14:4 _____

_____,

Paul indicates that the exercise of this gift could become a selfish experience. If so, then the gift is suspect as genuine.

Performance of the gift of speaking in tongues has a serious thread of causing divisions. Certain movements major on the performing of this gift, whether other believers agree with its use or not. Ephesians 4:3 states _____

_____

_____.

The Spirit causes believers to be in unity with one another whether or not the gift of tongues is exercised. Look at 1 Corinthians 14:33a: _____

_____.

Some believers have indicated time after time that the exercise of the gift of tongues can be a constant source of divisions. "It tends to create a tension between the 'haves' and the 'have nots,' and the impression is given, not always intentionally, that the 'have nots' are second-class Christians."[2]

In 1 Corinthians 14:14-15, Paul states _____

_____

_____.

From this we can detect that speaking in tongues is also one way to pray. Paul also states that it isn't even the best way to pray because "his understanding is unfruitful." Compare 1 Corinthians 14:14-17 with 1 Timothy 2:1 and write down the differences the Holy Spirit reveals to you concerning the two types of prayer. _____

_____

_____

_____

_____

_____

_____

With all of the other forms of prayer, speaking in tongues is the only form of prayer in which the intellect is not used.

II. DEFECTS CAUSED BY SPEAKING IN TONGUES

There are numerous spiritual defects that can be caused by the exercising of tongues-speaking. Divisions are possible, and a preoccupation with self is another. But there are others we will look into at this point.

1. Spiritual pride and a condescending attitude are evidences that there are defects in a believer's life. Others who do not possess the gift are looked at as if they are not "full" Christians. The exercising of tongues is not the only gift that causes "spiritual pride," but if a believer is immature, this gift will cause his/her "head" to swell.

2. Those with this gift tend to proselytize others to experience it also. The defect comes when the gift of tongues becomes more important to share than the Giver of tongues. If Christ becomes less important than the experience of speaking in tongues, then the gift should be suspect as to whether it is genuine. Nothing should take the place of Christ, not even the gifts He can give.

3. Some teach that speaking in tongues is the only evidence of being baptized in the Spirit. This is not supported Scripturally because the gifts of the Spirit are given to believers at the moment of conversion, as well as the baptism or filling of the Spirit. The exercising of the gifts can be done with or without the filling (control) of the Spirit. Therefore, speaking in tongues cannot be considered evidence of being baptized or filled. We are also told to "covet the best gifts," and tongues-speaking is considered a lesser gift. 1 Cor. 12:31a _____

_____.

In 1 Corinthians 14:39, the gift of tongues is at best not forbidden to be used _____

_____.

4. The example of the church that exercised the gift of tongues was a spiritually immature church that consisted of factions, immorality, cliques, and other excesses. Paul wrote in 1 Corinthians 3:1, _____

_____.

We are not to imitate babies in the Christian life. The use of this gift shows that you do not have to be spiritually mature to possess or exercise it. There is a genuine gift of tongues that exists but in order to exercise it, one does not have to be at the height of spiritual maturity.

5. Speaking in tongues can be counterfeited. The devil and his demons are able to imitate genuine works of God. Because the spiritual world and the physical world are tied closely together, we have to judge all experiences by Scripture rather than letting our experiences judge Scripture. Satan can counterfeit all of the gifts of the Spirit, and speaking in tongues is not exempt from his ability to imitate. Be careful when the gift is exercised, for if it does not follow Scriptural guidelines, then it could be counterfeit and should be dealt with according to Scripture.

III. DOES SCRIPTURE VALIDATE SPEAKING IN TONGUES AS EVIDENCE OF BEING BAPTIZED / FILLED WITH THE SPIRIT?

There are three occurrences in the Book of Acts that give clear light as to whether speaking in tongues is essential to being baptized or filled. Some teach that it is essential and that without it baptism in the Spirit is not experienced. The Scripture used is Acts 2:4, 10:46, and 19:16, where the baptism in the Spirit was followed by speaking in tongues. When closely studied, we find that "(1) a distinctive religious group was involved, and (2) there was a significant reason for the giving of this gift."[3]

1. Acts 2:4 _____

_____

_____.

As we discover from the surrounding passage, the feast of Pentecost was at hand, and a multitude of people were in Jerusalem to celebrate the occasion. Many were Jews, who regarded this feast as high and holy. It was fifty days after the Passover and the crucifixion. Ten days earlier Jesus had ascended back to the Father and had given His disciples specific instructions to "wait in Jerusalem until endued with power from on high." While 120 believers waited in the upper room, the crowds were gathering for the morning, and the Spirit Himself descended in three signs, (1) a rushing, mighty wind; (2) divided (cloven) tongues as of fire; and (3) utterances in other tongues. When the Spirit's descent was heard outside, the crowd came together and became confused because each person heard the disciples speak in his own language.

What was heard? Probably not the gospel, but in verse 11, it is stated they heard the disciples speak "the wonderful works of God." It seems no one came to Christ as a result of the speaking in tongues, but they became a captive audience for Peter's preaching the gospel. The result of the speaking in tongues was the attention of the crowd to hear the message of the gospel. The result of the message was three thousand souls saved.

From this expositional study of the Scripture, we find that the giving of tongues was evidence of the *gift* of the Spirit, not the *presence* of the Spirit, which drew attention to the proclamation of the gospel. Also, there is no record that the three thousand who were converted on that day spoke in tongues when they received salvation and the Spirit. Therefore, the main emphasis is not on the occurrence of tongues but on the proclamation of the gospel. The religious group was the Jews who always seemed to need a sign in order to believe. God gave them what they needed in order to receive Christ.

2. Acts 10:46 _____
_____.

In this passage, Peter was an unwilling servant when it came to serving others who were different from him. He religiously did not want to associate with any Gentiles, and the Lord had to give him specific directions that what He had to give was for *all* people, not merely a select group. Peter was an example of what was expected even in the new church. So when Christ gave the order to go, He wanted Peter to know that the same Spirit given to the Jews was also for the Gentiles and as he (Peter) had experienced speaking in tongues at Pentecost, Cornelius's experience was the same. It was the identical gift, and it gave evidence that God was not a respecter of persons (Acts 10:34 _____
_____).

It gave Peter and the other believers assurance that Gentile believers were the same in God's sight. Gentile believers were the religious group.

3. Acts 19:6 _____
_____.

In this passage, the disciples of John were unaware of the Person of the Holy Spirit when Paul asked them if they had received the Spirit when they believed. When Paul explained and laid hands on them, they received the same gift, and the evidence was that they spoke in tongues like the disciples and Cornelius. The Spirit came on them like He did at Pentecost, and they spoke in tongues likewise. It was never evidence of the presence of the Spirit but evidence of the gift of tongues.

4. Acts 8:17 _____
_____.

"It is not stated that speaking in tongues accompanied the

reception of the Spirit by the Samaritans, but some maintain that this is implied in the statement, 'When Simon SAW that the Spirit was given . . .' This is not in the text concerning tongues, but if it were true, here was another distinct religious group with whom the Jews had no dealings, and there would be the same reason for bestowing the gift of tongues as in the cases of the Gentiles."[4]

IV. SUMMARY

As we summarize this lesson, we come to the conclusion that none of the persons who spoke in tongues sought the experience. The group of disciples at Pentecost received the gift, and yet Cornelius as an individual also received the same gift. The overwhelming evidence points to the fact that experiences were evidences of the gift of tongues and not evidence of the presence of the Spirit. In the Ephesus account, they received the gift of tongues as well as the gift of prophecy. Therefore, if tongues were a sign of the baptism, then prophecy is to be included as well.

J. Oswald Sanders, in his book, *The Holy Spirit and His Gifts,* states, "It is to be noted that in no case did the recipients seek this gift, it was bestowed sovereignly. It was bestowed on the entire groups of people and individuals. In each case it came unexpectedly. In each case it was given at one and the same meeting. In each case it was present at the beginning of their Christian experience. There is no specific evidence that any of those who participated ever spoke in tongues again, although of course they may have done so. But the only other record of tongue-speaking is in the Church at Corinth.

"In these cases the gift of tongues was given as evidence that the identical gift of the Spirit had been bestowed on each group, not as evidence of the baptism or filling of the Spirit. If it were, that would make it the most important spiritual gift, and to be sought above all others. Paul's emphasis, however, is in the opposite direction. Prophecy is everywhere given precedence over tongues."[5]

LESSON 45

Further Gifts of the Spirit   Part XIX

Tongues—3

They all began to speak with other tongues . . . (Acts 2:4).

And to another the effecting of miracles . . . to another various kinds of tongues . . . (1 Cor. 12:10).

AIM: To discuss in detail the gift of tongues and how it relates to the believer

INTRODUCTION: As we have stated before, there has been a renewal of interest in the gift of "speaking in tongues." We have tried to examine in detail, in the light of Scripture, this gift. It would be impossible to cover all of the experiences that surround the exercising of the gift of tongues. The reason is that most people who are proselyting others have a subjective experience as the basis of their authority. Let's look at a few more aspects concerning the gift of speaking in tongues.

LESSON:

I. SIGNIFICANT OMISSIONS

We have noted before that beyond the experiences of tongues-speaking in Acts, there is no mention of the gift itself. We are to note that in the occurrences in Acts where speaking in tongues did occur, they did not coincide with the filling of the Spirit. Scripture records nine events of the filling of the Spirit, and at Pentecost was the only event where speaking in tongues resulted. Speaking in tongues is not recorded where Peter spoke before the Sanhedrin in Acts 4:8 _____

_____

_____,

neither when the believers were in prayer together in Acts 4:31

_____

_____.

When the seven deacons were appointed by the church there was no accompanying of speaking in tongues. Acts 6:5

_____

_____

_____.

In Acts 7:55, _____

_____,

when Stephen was giving his defense, there was no speaking in tongues, even though there was evidence of the filling of the Spirit. Also, in Acts 13:9, _____

_____,

Paul was filled with the Spirit, yet he did not speak in tongues. At his baptism in Acts 9:17 _____

_____,

again, the same evidence that speaking tongues does not coincide with the filling of the Spirit. Another incident in Acts 13:52

_____

_____,

also gives the same evidence.

At Pentecost, there is no mention of the 3,000 converts ever speaking in tongues, and their experience would coincide with most believers today. The majority of those reported as being saved are not reported as also speaking in tongues.

When it comes to an investigation of the Spirit-filled life, none of the Epistles mention tongues-speaking as an integral part of living for Christ. As a matter of fact it is totally ignored outside of 1 Corinthians 12, where Paul gives it a low priority. Paul referred to it as a gift that not every believer had and that was not an essential sign of receiving the Holy Spirit. If God had intended for it to be so important that all believers should experience it, He would have led Paul to say so.

II. RULES GOVERNING EXERCISE OF THE GIFT OF SPEAKING IN TONGUES

Paul did not question the validity of the gift of tongues. However, he knew there were some hidden dangers involved in its use. If there is genuine tongues-speaking, it must conform to the requirements of Scripture. As Paul advises the use of the gift, certain facts rise to the surface:

1. The giving of gifts is the right only of the Holy Spirit. As a result of this, we cannot demand any particular gift as a right of ours. 1 Cor. 12:11 _____

   _____.

2. There is no Scriptural mandate stating that all believers should or could speak in tongues. 1 Cor. 12:30 _____

   _____

   _____.

3. Paul encourages us to desire the best or greater gifts, which are to be used to edify the church. 1 Cor. 14:12 _____

   _____.

4. According to 1 Corinthians 14:12, _____

   _____,

   any gift given by the Spirit is to be used for edification of the body of Christ.

5. In order for a person who has a gift to tongues to exercise his gift, he must determine if a person with the gift of interpretation is there. 1 Cor. 14:28 _____

   _____

   _____.

6. As stated earlier, the gift of tongues was to be confined to only two or three people. They must speak in succession and not simultaneously. If it was not exercised in this man-

ner, it was not to be exercised at all, revealing that the gift of tongues could be controlled. 1 Cor. 14:27 _____

_____.

7. If when exercising the gift of tongues, confusion resulted, it was a possible sign that it was not a genuine experience. 1 Cor. 14:33 _____

_____.

8. All gifts of the Spirit created harmony and peace. The Spirit is a Spirit of unity. Whatever creates division should be handled with suspicion. Eph. 4:3 _____

_____

_____.

III. SUMMARY

Here are several summary facts, taken from *A Guide to Knowing God* by Michael K. Haynes, concerning the gift of tongues.

1. "The tongues spoken at Pentecost were known languages. Acts 2:1-12.

2. "The New Testament gift of tongues was given by God as a sign to the Jews. Acts 2:1-12.

3. "The church at Corinth was misusing and abusing the gifts of the Spirit and there was the false or counterfeit among them also. 1 Cor. 12—14. Many people today want to base their doctrine upon a letter that was written to correct an error. The Corinthians were in error. Paul wrote to correct them.

4. "There are those who say that everyone must have the gift of tongues in order to be filled or baptized with the Holy Spirit. This is not scriptural truth. 1 Cor. 12:4-7,29-30.

5. "God is sovereign. He can give anything to anyone He chooses.

6. "The biblical value of speaking in tongues is found in 1 Corinthians 14. It actually places little value upon the gift of speaking in tongues. More emphasis is usually given to

the subjective experience of tongue-speaking than about Jesus or the inspired Word of God.

7. "Sometimes praying in the Spirit as recorded in Ephesians 6:18 is used to back up the value of the gift. Paul tells others to make specific requests for him to God that he may speak boldly. You cannot make specific requests if you do not know what you are saying. Paul labels this kind of prayer as unfruitful.

8. "Pagan religions have always had forms of tongue-speaking involved. Corinth was a center for other religions and had some influence on the Christian church.

9. "Some have said that speaking in tongues is the kind of experience everyone should seek because '. . . it is the objectivity for one's continued walk in the Spirit.'

10. "The Devil can give false experiences of speaking in tongues. It can also be 'worked up' by a person's will power. There are many references to the gift of tongues in the Bible. Listed below are a few references. Look them up and record your own insights as to this gift.

    1. Acts 2:1-11 _____

    _____

    _____

    _____.

    2. Acts 10:44-46_____

    _____

    _____

    _____.

    3. Acts 10:1-6_____

    _____

    _____

    _____.

    4. 1 Cor. 12:1-14_____

    _____

_____

_____.

5. 1 Cor. 14:1-40"[1] _____

_____

_____

_____.

LESSON 46

Further Gifts of the Spirit   Part XX

Interpretation of Tongues

And to another . . . the interpretation of tongues . . . (1 Cor. 12:10).

AIM: To give additional insight in regards to the interpretation of tongues and how it relates to the believer

INTRODUCTION: From Scripture we determined that the goal of any spiritual gift is to edify the body of Christ. The gift of tongues was given to the Corinthian church with certain restrictions as we discussed in Lessons 43-45. Included in these restrictions is the gift of interpretation of tongues. Let's look at this gift to find out some aspects of its use in the church.

LESSON:

I. DEFINITION

The Greek word for the interpretation of tongues is *hermeneia,* from which we derive the word interpretation. It means to explain the meaning of words in a different language, as in 1 Corinthians 12:10 _____

_____,

and 14:26 _____

_____.

The Greek word *glossa,* from which we get tongues or language, means in the New Testament the Spirit-given gift of speaking in another language without learning it.

As we have discussed in an earlier lesson, in Acts 2:4-13 the

187

experience of tongues was from the viewpoint of those who heard them. What they heard from the disciples was either from drunkards or supernaturally motivated believers who were lead to speak "the mighty works of God."

In 1 Corinthians 12 and 14, the exercising of tongues was limited to the local congregation. Specifically, in 1 Corinthians 12:10, the gift of tongues is tied to the gift of interpretation of tongues. In Chapter 14, however, Paul gave specific instructions on the exercising of tongues, which again was limited to the edification of the church.

II. RESTRICTIONS OF TONGUES WITH INTERPRETATION

Paul states in 1 Corinthians 14:4-6: _____

_____

_____

_____ ,

that unless tongues were interpreted by a person with the gift of interpretation, the person who gave the utterance of the tongue or language would be speaking to God and not to men. In verse 2, Paul also states that the speaker of a tongue would edify himself and not the church. If there were no person to interpret the utterance of a tongue, the person with the gift of tongues was to keep silent.

III. OTHER RESTRICTIONS

From Scripture, speaking tongues in a church was to be limited to only two or three persons, and each was to speak in turn. Each was to speak in succession but never at the same time. When believers violated these Scriptural guidelines, the tongues were to be stopped as an indication that the gift of tongues could be controlled.

IV. SUMMARY

There is not much to be known concerning the gift of interpretation of tongues. It was the supernatural ability to translate unknown languages of those who had the gift of tongues. However, the gift of tongues and interpretation of tongues have become controversial because of modern movements toward speaking in tongues. Today, leaders and teachers are training others how to speak in tongues and how to interpret them. However, according to Scripture, spiritual gifts are not taught but are given by the Holy Spirit as He sees fit. As a result, divisions often occur in fellowships where tongues are being taught as an evidence of being filled with the Spirit. Look up Ephesians 4:11-13 and determine from your own study what the purpose of gifts are for the believer._____

_____

_____

_____

LESSON 47

Further Gifts of the Spirit   Part XXI

Healings

And to another the effecting of miracles, . . . then the gifts of healings, . . . (1 Cor. 12:10,28).

AIM: To discuss in detail the gift of healings and how it relates to the believer

INTRODUCTION: The gift of healing is given by the Holy Spirit. It literally means acts of healing or cures. Throughout the Bible, cases of healing appear. In the New Testament specifically, there are numerous miracles of healing by Jesus and His disciples. Throughout history, people have been healed, and such is documented. However, it has sometimes been associated with faith healers. Many of these so-called "healers" claim to have this gift, and thousands of people run to them for healing. As a result of this popularity, the church has had a tremendous light of controversy placed upon it.

No one living can escape all sickness indefinitely. All people eventually die, including faith healers. We will look briefly at the Scriptural gift of healing to determine its authenticity in today's world.

LESSON:

I. DEFINITION

The gift of healing is the supernatural ability to restore instantly health to a mind or body. The word healing comes from the Greek words *charismata iamaten* and means "the act of

190

healing or the gift of cures." The one who possessed this gift was able to go before the person who was sick and, by exercising his faith toward God, he could declare healing. This gift was the supernatural intervention of God through a person. As we study Scripture, not all cases of sickness were healed. Only God is the One who determines when and where healing is effected. He does not make specific promises to every believer that He will heal them. Although Paul had the gift of healing, he could not heal everybody he came into contact with. In 2 Timothy 4:20, _____

_____,

Paul was unable to heal Trophimus. In 1 Timothy 5:23,

_____

_____,

Paul advised Timothy to take a little medicinal wine for his "stomach's sake." Also, Paul himself had an infirmity that was not healed. He even prayed to the Lord about it in 2 Corinthians 12:7-8: _____

_____.

II. CONTROVERSIES CONCERNING CLAIMS OF HEALING

There are often controversial claims concerning healing in some doctrinal teaching. Some snatch certain Scriptures out of context in order to foster their teaching. Listed below are some of those claims and controversies.

1. Some teach a "Name-It-Claim-It" doctrine. The error of this teaching lies in the fact that, "God does not will perfect health and complete healing for every believer. They also teach that God has obligated Himself to heal every sickness for those who have faith."[1]

2. Some teach that healing is included in the atonement. They use Isaiah 53:5, _____

_____,

to teach that Isaiah was speaking of physical healing. He was not speaking of physical sicknesses but of spiritual sicknesses. The context of the verse sheds this light. Isaiah was sharing that the Christ would suffer the death of a cross and thereby provide cleansing from all spiritual sicknesses. In Christ there is instant healing for a sin-sick soul.

3. Some teach that all sickness is the result of sin in a believer's life or because of satanic activity. Some adamantly believe that if a person is ill, either there is sin in their lives or Satan is active in them. If it were simply because of sin in our lives that we are sick, all we would have to do to remedy the situation is to confess our sin, and healing would or should be the result. First John 1:9, _____

_____,

gives a solution for the sin problem, but it does not promise results of physical healing if done.

III. SUMMARY

There is a legitimate gift of healing. The results of people praying in faith and receiving an answer of healing are not disputed. However, the danger in "healing services" is that people tend to spotlight the gift or the person but rarely the Divine Healer. He is the One Who is sovereign in His acts, and his acts may or may not be evident in healing. He is able to do exactly what He wants to do. His ways, however, are not our ways, for they are far above our thoughts. We are to think more of the Giver than the gift.

LESSON 48

How to Recognize Your Gift

And He gave some as apostles, and some as prophets, and some as evangelists, and some as pastors and teachers, for the equipping of the saints for the work of service, to the building up of the body of Christ (Eph. 4:11-12).

AIM: To show how a person who does not yield to his/her gift and his/her place will be like a nut and bolt that is the wrong size and a mechanic that tries to make it work (The end result is always total frustration.)

INTRODUCTION: The Holy Spirit is the Source of gifts that are given to believers at the moment of salvation. Each new believer has his/her own distinct gift or gifts. Paul outlines in 1 Corinthians 12 that "the body is not one member but many." He states that some are feet, some are hands, some eyes, others are ears, and still others are legs. The common denominator connected with all the members of the body is that they are in *one body* and available to the entire body to function as intended. Each member is designed to produce a part of a whole body in order that the head is satisfied.

The point of this lesson as outlined by Paul is that the human body is designed with many parts, each working to the betterment of the whole body. This is the spiritual analogy involved in the physical church.

As it relates to the Spiritual Body, are you a hand or a foot, maybe an ear or eye, possibly a tongue or arm? What is your

193

spiritual gift? How do you recognize your gift? Let's look together at some general principles that will help you to find out
your spiritual gift(s).

There are several prerequisites in order to find out your spiritual gift.

1. *You have to be a born-again believer.* A person must have
   accepted Christ as his personal Lord and Savior. Without
   Christ in a person's life, there is no need for a spiritual gift,
   for that person is not a part of the body of Christ.

2. *There must be no habitual sin in your life.* Any sin will hinder
   the Spirit's revelation of spiritual truths in our lives. Habitual
   sins hinder our effectiveness to perform once we become
   aware of our gift.

3. *You must determine your desires for a spiritual gift.* Your motives play a vital part as to the performance of a particular
   gift. Selfish motives hinder the Spirit's effectiveness through
   you.

I. A BELIEVER WILL HAVE A SPIRIT-LED INCLINATION TO BE OF SERVICE TO OTHERS IN THAT AREA

How does an eye develop into an eye? It starts "seeing" as it
continues to develop. How does a person become a singer?
Their voice begins to develop, and there is an inner awareness
of a gift taking shape. There is a desire to be of service to others
in that area.

II. A BELIEVER'S GIFT MAY BE THE PROPHECY OF SOME OTHER "GIFTED PERSON OF GOD"

According to 2 Timothy 1:6-7, _____

_____

_____,

the laying on of hands could very well be their "pointing out of
that gift publicly." Seek out a person whom you trust and respect as a spiritual authority for their insight. Sometimes God

gives them insight to help confirm your spiritual gift. This alone is not enough to determine your gift. You must take all principles into consideration.

III. A BELIEVER'S GIFT, WHEN EXERCISED, WILL BRING HIM/HER A SENSE OF SATISFACTION

You will feel comfortable doing it. It is possible to write with a pen between your toes instead of your fingers. However, it will not feel comfortable. From this illustration, which one is the natural gift to write with? Your gift will bring great joy and satisfaction to you when you exercise it. If you do not enjoy teaching, then it may not be your gift. If you like to help, and it brings satisfaction and joy, then it could be your gift.

IV. A BELIEVER'S GIFT WILL CAUSE OTHERS TO BE BLESSED BECAUSE OF IT

One way for a believer to know he may not have a gift in a particular area is: when he exercises his "gift," others wish he wouldn't. If a surgeon has a "gift" to operate, then he does not "lose all of his patients on the operating table." Others will receive a blessing from you when your gift is exercised. If they are not blessed, and sense selfish motives from you, then that may not be your gift, or you are operating for self and not the Savior.

Concerning your gift: 2 Tim. 1:6-7 _____

_____

_____

_____

_____.

V. SUMMARY

How do we recognize our gift(s)? Use all of the above principles to help you. If that fails, here are five conclusions that could help you as the Spirit leads.

1. *Be informed about all of the gifts of the Spirit.* Use Lessons 27-47 as a guide.

2. *Be open to the Spirit as He leads you to one of the lesser desired gifts.* Not everyone is called to be a pastor or an evangelist. Some have the gifts of helps, encouragement, and the like. Be open.

3. *Be available when an opportunity to serve arises.* It may be the avenue by which the Spirit leads to show you your gift.

4. *Be sensitive to meeting needs instead of letting your desire to know your spiritual gift have top priority.* Never let your desire to know your gift stop you from ministering. You could very well hinder the Spirit's leading by being insensitive to other believers.

5. *Be sensible as it relates to serving.* Serve whether you have a particular gift or not. If asked to do so, trust other's judgment of you. The worst you can do is fail. However, in strategic areas, be sensible enough to let others know you have no experience in that area and forgo the excitement of the moment for a less visible moment of trial and error.

LESSON 49

Sins Against the Holy Spirit Part I

Grieving the Holy Spirit

And do not grieve the Holy Spirit of God, by whom you were sealed for the day of redemption (Eph. 4:30).

AIM: To discuss the sins against the Holy Spirit that are committed by believers only

INTRODUCTION: E. H. Hopkins says, "When sin comes into my life it displeases the Holy Spirit, He reproves me; but lets me never forget that it pains Him. He hates sin, and it pains Him because He sees that by sinning I lose His blessing, it does injury to my soul."[1] This is one of the proofs of the personality of the Holy Spirit. Sinning against Him is a serious offense, and its magnitude is determined by the character of the Holy Spirit and not by the sin itself. He is divine in nature and equal with the Father and Son.

Therefore, every offense against Him is very serious. As a matter of information, the only sin that receives no forgiveness is committed against the Spirit alone. The sins which cause the most grief to the Holy Spirit are classified into two categories: believers grieving or quenching the Spirit. Only the unbeliever may blaspheme the Spirit. Part I in this three-part series will deal with grieving the Holy Spirit; Part II, with quenching the Spirit; and Part III, with the unpardonable sin.

LESSON:

I. GRIEVING THE HOLY SPIRIT

"And do not grieve the Holy Spirit of God." This phrase oc-

197

curs once in the Bible and means "to cause sorrow to." The fact that we can make the Spirit grieve should make us sensitive to sin and cause us to watch our actions, attitudes, and ambitions. Not all Christians are aware of the amount of grief they cause the Spirit by their sinning.

"Grieve is a love word. One can anger an enemy, but not grieve him. Only one who loves can be grieved, and the deeper the love the greater the grief. How gracious the Spirit has been to us who have 'grieved Him by a thousand falls.'"[2]

Ephesians 4:30 can be translated "cease grieving the Spirit," or "Do not have the habit of grieving the Spirit."[3] If there is an area in our lives that grieves the Spirit, we must deal with it. If we do not, we will fall into the habit of grieving Him as a way of life.

II. WHAT GRIEVES THE SPIRIT?

The command to "grieve not the Spirit" occurs between a list of sins of communication and sins of action which grieve the Spirit. First Corinthians 6:19 states, _____

_____.

Because of the presence of the Spirit, He makes one's body a temple. As a result of his being within us, any sin in our lives grieves Him. We should invite the Spirit to search our hearts and let His spotlight uncover any sin that grieves Him. As we go through this study, let Him guide you as you discover areas that need to be dealt with.

1. One way we grieve the Holy Spirit is by "ignoring His indwelling presence. Some Christians live as if there were no Holy Spirit. From Sunday morning to Saturday night they give not one thought of conscious recognition to the Spirit."[4] The Spirit does not like to be ignored, and you and I do not appreciate it either. To counter the ignoring of the Spirit, we should spend enough time each day becoming aware of His presence.

2. The Spirit becomes grieved when we "change His commands." When we do not follow the biblical blueprint that He designed through His Word, we cause Him to grieve. Specifically, when He says "Go!" and we stay, then He is grieved. When we choose not to obey His commands and His will, He withholds His activity and fellowship, and we no longer are in full fellowship with Christ.

III. SPECIFIC SINS THAT GRIEVE THE HOLY SPIRIT

There are specific sins which cause the grieving of the Spirit. They are found in Ephesians 4:25-29 _____

_____

_____.

Paul states that we are to "put away lying." The Greek word is *pseudos*, which means anything false. We are admonished to *"be angry and sin not,"* which does not command us to be angry but indicates there is a danger of sinning when we are angry, and that grieves the Holy Spirit. We are further encouraged: "Let not the sun go down upon thy wrath" (KJV). In other words, we are not to let our anger brew within us until we blow up and grieve the Spirit as a result. When we allow our anger to develop and be carried into another day, forgiveness is hard to be reached.

Paul also states that "he that steals is to steal no more." The principle is honesty. We are to be honest and trustworthy in our daily lives because it is a reflection on Christ when we fail in our testimony before others. There are no degrees of honesty. Either you can be trusted with little or much or you cannot be trusted with either. To counteract a life of dishonesty, we are to labor, providing for our own needs with our own abilities.

Paul further suggests: "Let no corrupt communication proceed out of your mouth." Anything that is corrupt is "rotten, putrid" like fish that has spoiled. The aroma that proceeds from the spoiled fish is definitely corrupt, and all who come near become aware of it—like the corrupt talk that can spew from our mouths. The odor informs others that it is rotten, putrid, and is not worthy of a child of God. The antidote for corrupt talk is "that which is good to the use of edifying, that it may minister grace unto the hearers." Do not let the Spirit be grieved by your language and behavior.

We are also told to let all "bitterness, wrath, anger, clamor, and evil speaking" be put away from us. These sins cause deep grief to the Holy Spirit, whether He is ignored, disobeyed, or when His commands are violated.

IV. SIX SIGNS AS TO WHEN THE HOLY SPIRIT IS GRIEVED

1. *A person will lose interest in studying the Bible on a daily basis.* Consistent Bible study habits will not develop. To the contrary, the emphasis on the Word will be deemphasized by a believer who grieves the Spirit. Illumination and revelation through the Word of God are totally dependent upon the teaching ministry of the Holy Spirit, and when He is grieved, it shortcircuits His lines of communication.

2. *A person's prayer life will be poor or almost nonexistent.* Prayers will become long and lifeless when the Spirit is grieved. He is the only One upon whom the inspiration of prayer is dependent. Without Him, prayers will go no further than the ceiling of our prayer closets until we deal with what grieves Him. 1 John 1:9, _____

_____

_____.

3. *A person will not experience victory over sin, and past victories will become memories of times that were.* When the Spirit is grieved, our ability to overcome temptations diminishes and makes us an open target for the attacks of Satan. Without the "law of the Spirit of life," Romans 8:2,

_____

_____,

which makes us free from the law of sin and death, we are left with our own power to overcome the wiles of Satan and we are no match for his power. The result is always loss of victory over sin.

4. *A person will begin to be aware of a loss of Christ's presence in his life.* Only the Spirit within can make Christ's presence real to us. When we grieve Him, the awareness of His presence will fade. We will feel left alone, abandoned. It is not that He has withdrawn but that we have.

5. *A person will begin to question his assurance of salvation.* The Spirit bears witness with our spirits that we are the children of God. When we grieve Him, we begin to question the new creation that He started in us at salvation. Grieving causes loss of fellowship, which gives a sense of loss of relationship, but we actually never lose our relationship once we have been born again.

6. *A person will also lose supernatural power to perform service.* A person will keep the gifts the Spirit has bestowed upon him/her, but the fruit of the Spirit will not be as apparent in daily living.

Though a person will not lose his salvation by grieving the Spirit, he will begin to lose the usefulness he has experienced before.

V. DOES THE SPIRIT WITHDRAW WHEN HE IS GRIEVED?

When we grieve the Spirit, He is saddened by our taking control of our lives. He becomes a passenger on the bus of our lives, while we do all of the driving. He has more experience at driving a life than we, but does He get off of the bus when we take over? Some of our hymns suggest that He does or can withdraw, but this is not a biblical concept. David prayed in Psalm 51:11*b*: _____,
before the Holy Spirit came to indwell believers at Pentecost. But we are not to pray this prayer because, once the Spirit is

within us, He never leaves. What then does He do when we grieve Him? He does, however, withdraw His influence and power—but never His presence. When we grieve Him, we shut out and exclude His ministry in our lives, and we hinder His desire of revealing Christ to us. He, though, does not withdraw His total influence, for He uses His love for us to reveal our sin in order that we may confess and be restored to full fellowship with Him.

VI. IS THERE A SOLUTION?

Is there anything we can do to restore the fellowship with the Spirit that has grown stale and stagnant? The only solution is 1 John 1:9. The biblical mandate on confession of sins states that the sin (of commission or omission) should be confessed to the one against whom it was committed. If it has been against God alone, then confession should be made to God alone. If against others, then it should be confessed both to the person involved, as well as to God, and restitution should be made where necessary. If the sin was committed publicly, then confession should be public. If committed privately, then confession should be private. As a result of this, the Holy Spirit will again take the reins of your life and continue to mold you into the image of Christ.

VII. SUMMARY

Any sin in a believer's life will grieve the Holy Spirit. When this happens, a person should pray similar to this:

Dear Lord Jesus,

I (we) confess that I (we) have sinned against you (and another, if it is the case) and ask the You forgive me (us) according to 1 John 1:9 that says that if I (we) will confess my (our) sins, You are faithful and just to forgive me (us) and cleanse me (us) from all unrighteousness. I (we) ask in faith right now that You do what you said and fill me (us) again with Your precious Holy Spirit that He may again take control and give me (us) power to live a life of service that is pleasing to You. I (we) thank You right now for doing this in my (our) life (lives).

In Jesus' Name,

LESSON 50

Sins Against the Holy Spirit   Part II

Quenching the Spirit

Do not quench the Spirit; . . . (1 Thess. 5:19).

AIM: To discuss the sins against the Holy Spirit that are committed by believers only

INTRODUCTION: The Bible is filled will illustrations of the Holy Spirit as a symbol of fire. To "quench" means to put out as of a fire or thirst. Therefore, the Scripture above can be paraphrased, "Do not extinguish the Spirit's fire," as rendered in the Berkley Bible. Thayer suggests that it means "to suppress or stifle." In our Scripture, this sin would consist of trying to suppress or put out the influence of the Holy Spirit's presence.

LESSON:

I. WHAT DOES QUENCHING DEAL WITH?

From 1 Thessalonians 5:19, we deduce that the "quenching" of the Spirit's influence was related to His public ministry in the church rather than in the private lives of the believers. Verses 12-23 suggest this context. In Matthew 3:11, _____

_____

_____,

John the Baptist prophesied that, "He shall baptize you with the Holy Spirit and with fire." Our responsibility then is not to allow actions, attitudes, or ambitions of ours "put out" the Holy Spirit's fire. It is evident that in Thessalonica, members of the church

were trying to "put out" the fire of the Holy Spirit by despising spiritual gifts. 1 Thess. 5:20: _____.
The ministry of the Spirit through His many gifts is not to be guarded, but unhindered, whether in the church or in an individual believer's life.

II. HOW MAY WE QUENCH HIM?

Billy Graham suggests that there are two basic ways of quenching a fire:
1. "Removing the fuel supply.
2. Extinguishing it, by throwing water on it or smothering it with a blanket or a shovel full of dirt."[1]

We quench the influence of the Spirit in our own lives by failing to answer His directions for our involvement in service or in giving testimonies. We also fail by not taking opportunities for ministry that He so carefully orchestrates on our behalf. When we deny Him the fuel of prayer, Bible study, free-hearted giving, holy living, and the like, His fire in our lives is diminished.

We can also quench the Spirit in the lives of other believers by criticizing them, being unkind, showing ingratitude of their contribution to the kingdom, no matter how little, and in other ways. The Spirit's influence can also be quenched by a corporate action of the church. Many a church has stifled the movement of the Spirit in their ministry through divisions, formalism, manipulation, and cliques. 1 Cor. 1:10-11, _____

_____

_____.

III. IS THERE A SOLUTION?

Again, as stated in the previous lesson, the only solution is 1 John 1:9. Confession is needed to restore fellowship with God and with others. The suggested prayer given in the previous lesson is appropriate to restore the fellowship of the family of God. Corporate action should be done on the same level of confession—all!

IV. SUMMARY

There are two other hindrances which quench the ministry of the Holy Spirit in the life of a believer. The first is resisting the Spirit (Acts 7:51 _____

_____);

and lying to the Spirit (Acts 5:3 _____

_____).

In resisting the Spirit, the unbeliever is also capable of committing this offense. In the above Scripture, Stephen in his defense warned the crowd that they were guilty of doing what their forefathers had done: resisting the leading of the Holy Spirit. God has marvelous works to perform in the lives of unbelievers as well as believers. Believers can also resist the leading of the Spirit.

Lying to the Spirit is the other offense that believers should not commit. In Acts 5, Ananias and his wife Sapphira made a promise to the Spirit Himself. They were led to sell their land and to put the money into the common treasury of the church. They did not fulfill their promise to the Spirit and kept some of the money for themselves.

Peter's charge to Ananias and Sapphira was that they had not lied to men but to the Holy Spirit. They had the right to give what they wanted to give willingly, but because of the pretense of giving all, their testimony in giving was a lie. Because of the judgment upon them, fear fell upon the whole church. The people were afraid to go contrary to the will of God. God was moving in power, but Ananias and Sapphira were hindrances to His work, and as a result God moved them. This principle has been used at other times. When someone stands in the way of His ministry He can through judgment remove them. That is fearful to consider.

LESSON 51

Sins Against the Holy Spirit   Part III

The Unpardonable Sin

Therefore I say to you, any sin and blasphemy shall be forgiven men, but blasphemy against the Spirit shall not be forgiven. And whoever shall speak a word against the Son of Man, it shall be forgiven him; but whoever shall speak against the Holy Spirit, it shall not be forgiven him, either in this age, or in the age to come (Matt. 12:31-32).

AIM: To discuss specifically the unpardonable sin and how it relates to the believer

INTRODUCTION: René Paché, a Christian theologian in his work, *Reason and the Work of the Holy Spirit,* observed, "To sin against God under the law was a serious matter. The sin against Jesus Christ in human form was yet more serious" (John 15:22— _____

_____

_____);

"nevertheless the Son in His humility presented Himself in visible form to men, to repulse Him was still pardonable. But to resist the Spirit who glorifies Him and who gives rise within our hearts to an unmistakably clear conviction is an act of willful sin, willingly and deliberately shutting the door in the face of God. The work of the Spirit, seeking to place within us the Savior's presence, is the final issue in God's plan for us. If man rejects it and maintains his stubbornness, God can do no more for him; He cannot save him in opposition to his will."[1]

There is nothing more serious in this life or in the life to come as the issue of the unpardonable sin. This is a difficult subject to deal with in such a short lesson, but we will attempt to discover the implications and irrevocableness of this sin.

LESSON:

I. WHAT IS IT TO BLASPHEME?

"Blasphemy is contempt or indignity offered to God. It is to revile, slander, speak lightly or derogatorily of sacred things or persons. It is not only a sin of the lips, but comes out of the heart."[2] Matt. 15:9 _____

_____.

The Greek word for blasphemy is *blasphemeō,* which means "to defame, speak evil of, use abusive speech." In Ephesians 4:31 it is translated as "evil-speaking."

II. WHAT IS THE DIFFERENCE BETWEEN BLASPHEMING THE SPIRIT AND THE SON OF MAN?

There is no greater holiness in one Person of the Godhead than in another. However, Jesus offered forgiveness for every other sin, even the sin of blaspheming Him. What is the difference if both the Spirit and the Son are God? "Jesus does not use the title 'Son of God' of Himself, but 'Son of Man.' The Son of Man is God veiled in humanity, God incarnate. The Holy Spirit is God in majesty and glory. It was against Jesus as Son of Man the Pharisees had blasphemed, for they explicitly refused to accept His claim to be Son of God."[3] Matt. 12:34: _____

_____.

Paul also testified that he had blasphemed Jesus and that he had received forgiveness. 1 Tim. 1:13 _____

_____.

There is a vast difference between speaking abusively of the Son of man in His humanity and speaking abusively of Him after His resurrection and ascension and the descent of the

Spirit. Many of those who had spoken evil of Jesus when He was incarnate became faithful followers after Pentecost.

III. WHAT IS THE UNPARDONABLE SIN?

There are five different aspects as to what the unpardonable sin is and what it is not.

1. *"It is not a sin of ignorance, but a sin against spiritual knowledge and light. God has not set an invisible line where one may cross without knowing.*

2. *It is not an isolated act, but a habitual attitude, a sin in character, hardened in opposition to God.*

3. *It is a sin of the heart, and not merely of the intellect or tongue, an act of the will.*

4. *It is a sin committed in willful resistance to the working of the Spirit, a sin of presumption.*

5. *It is a sin committed by unbelievers only."*[4]

IV. WHY IS THERE NO FORGIVENESS FOR THIS SIN?

Are the death, burial, and resurrection of Christ insufficient to cover this sin? No. In order for there to be forgiveness, there have to be two persons, the forgiver and the one needing forgiveness. If a person has consistently refused to be forgiven, what else can be done? Forgiveness must be asked for and accepted in order for the transaction to be complete. This sin is unforgivable because it rejects forgiveness and as a result, there is no other provision. "It is unforgivable because it is, (Mark 3:29 _____

_____)

and its punishment is unending, because the sin is unending."[5]

V. SUMMARY

There can be no doubt as to the seriousness of blaspheming the Holy Spirit. The very fact Jesus taught that all manner of sin and blasphemy would be forgiven men, except the blasphemy against the Holy Spirit, shows what terrible wickedness God considers this sin to include. It is one that will not be forgiven in this age or in the age to come. This is a personal sin committed only by unbelievers.

If there is fear and concern over the matter of sin, it is likely that the Holy Spirit is still working in that person's life to bring him or her into a saving knowledge of Jesus Christ. A person who has committed the unpardonable sin has no feelings or emotions in the area of conviction of sin. He will be insensitive to any leading of the Spirit. There will be no desire, no longing, no leading by the Spirit. Persons like these are deaf to the voice of the Spirit and will not respond to Him.

Consequently, anyone who is afraid to having committed this sin, and is still outside the arch of safety of the cross, should know from the presence of fear that the Spirit is holding the door open to him or her to receive Christ.

LESSON 52

The Struggle Within

For that which I am doing, I do not understand, . . . which is in my members (Rom. 7:15,21,23).

AIM: To discuss the inner warfare that comes into the life of a born-again believer

INTRODUCTION: "An Eskimo fisherman came to town every Saturday afternoon. He always brought his two dogs with him. One was white and the other was black. He had taught them to fight on command. Every Saturday afternoon in the town square the people would gather and these two dogs would fight and the fisherman would take bets. On one Saturday the black dog would win. The next Saturday the white dog would win— but the fisherman always won! His friends began to ask him how he did it. He said, 'I starve one and feed the other. The one I feed always wins because he is stronger.'"[1]

This illustration gives us an idea of the inner struggle that goes on in the life of a believer. We have two natures within us, both trying to gain the superior role. Which one will rule? It depends on which one we feed. If we feed the spirit within us, he will rule. If we starve the spirit within, the flesh will rule.

To some Christians, the inner struggle is a maze of confusion because they assume that in accepting Christ, all their problems

211

are solved. The truth is that in becoming a believer, salvation underlines one's problems like a foundation of a building. No matter what structural problems there are, if the foundation is good, all other areas can be corrected. There's a well-known saying that "clothes make the man!" The truth of this statement may be debatable in real life, but in the spiritual life, it holds true. Paul in Ephesians 4:22-24 wrote: _____

_____

_____

_____.

The outfit we wear makes a big difference as to whether we are "putting off" the old or "putting on" the new. As a further analogy of the Christian life, before a person is converted, he has only one set of clothes from which to choose, all of which makes self stand out. By receiving Christ as personal Savior, the believer receives a new set of clothes that will represent Christ in his life. The struggle enters when we have to choose the "suit of self" or the "suit of Christ." Romans 7:15,21,23 gives us insight into this daily struggle.

The end result of this struggle within is called sanctification, or to be made holy (from the Greek word *hagiazō,* meaning "to be separate" or "set apart for a purpose"). It implies that we are continually saying "no" to self and "yes" to Christ—to the One who has set us apart for His purpose. If you are struggling within, it is a good sign there are two sets of clothes in your life; the choice is up to you as to which one you will wear—the old or the new. Whose ambassador will you be—self or Christ's? Remember 2 Corinthians 5:17 _____

_____

_____.

When the Bible speaks of "putting on" or "putting off," it is referring to what is produced in our lives. When we "put on," we are producing some aspect. When we "put off," we are to stop producing some aspect. What are some aspects we are to "put off" or stop producing? By doing so, the struggle within becomes less and less of a struggle. Let's look at Galatians 5:19-21 for our answer.

I. FOUR BRANCHES OF FLESHLY WORKS

In Galatians 5, Paul lists both the "clothes to put off" as well as the "clothes to put on." The clothes to put on are the "fruit of the Spirit," which we have already discussed in lessons 16-26, and need not be discussed here. Refer to them for further insight. The clothes that we are to "put off" are called the "works of the flesh." They are produced by the flesh alone. In verse 19-21, Paul outlines four "branches" or categories of "works" of the flesh. The four "branches" are: (1) sensual sins, (2) spiritual sins, (3) social sins, and (4) sins of excess. We will take a brief look at each branch.

II. SENSUAL SINS

1. *Immorality*. The Greek word for this is *porneia*, from which the word "pornography" comes. It is a general term used to include all kinds of sexual wickedness, from premarital sex to prostitution. Any deviation outside of marriage vows is the thought.

2. *Adultery*. The Greek word for this is *mioxeia*, which is simply having relations with someone else other than your marriage partner. This could be included in 1.

3. *Impurity*. The Greek word for this is *akathartos*, which suggests uncleanness in acts, attitudes, or ambitions. It includes Romans 1:24 _____

_____.

William Barclay describes it as the *"pus of an unclean wound; a tree that has never been pruned; material that has never been sifted."*[2] A. T. Robertson, in his *Word Pictures in the New Testament*, states that the impurity is moral in nature.

4. *Sensuality*. The Greek word for this is *aselgeia,* which means "wantonness" or "having no self-respect," "unrestrained living," or "unbridled acts of indescency which shock the public."[3]

III. SPIRITUAL SINS

1. *Idolatry*. The Greek word for this is *eidololatreia,* which means the worship of heathen gods or images. It includes anything that can take the place of or separate us from God.

2. *Sorcery*. The Greek word for this is *pharmakeia,* from which we get our word "pharmacy." It meant the use of drugs in witchcraft or "the use of medicine or drugs, the use of drugs for magical purposes, magic, sorcery."[4] Witchcraft and sorcery are condemned throughout Scripture.

IV. SOCIAL SINS

1. *Enmities*. The Greek word for this is *echthra,* which means "hostility." It could mean "hostilities between individuals, communities, based on political or religious grounds. Not only hostile acts are included, but the underlying emotions and intentions are also included."[5]

2. *Strife*. The Greek word for this is *ereis,* which means "quarrelsomeness"[6] or "contentions."[7]

3. *Jealousy*. The Greek word for this is *zelos,* which means "envying or malice."

4. *Anger*. The Greek word for this is *thumoi,* which means "fierceness, indignation, or wrath." Fritz Rienecker states that it means "a terrible flair up of temper."[8]

5. *Rivalries*. The Greek word for this is *eritheia,* which means "factions," or "selfishness, self-seeking ambition."[9] "This violates both parts of the Ten Commandments. First, it is a sin against God when selfish ambitions replace the will of God for our lives. Then it violates the command to love our

neighbors, for acts of self-seeking are always committed at someone else's expense."[10]

6. *Divisions.* The Greek word for this is *dichostasia,* which means "dissensions, division, or sedition." The only other occurrence of this word is found in Romans 16:17, where Paul warns the Romans against those who cause divisions. We are to be on guard that we do not become the instruments of division within the body of Christ.

7. *Heresies.* The Greek word for this is *hairesis,* which means "factions." It is the result of 6, "divisions organized into factions, cliques,"[11] leading to error in theological truths.

8. *Envyings.* The Greek word for this is *phthomeo,* which means "resentment at the excellence or good fortune of another, a jealous spirit."[12] "It is wholly evil, the spirit that cannot bear to contemplate someone else's prosperity."[13]

9. *Murders.* The Greek word for this is *phonoi,* which means "murder, slaughter." The idea is the taking of another life.

V. SINS OF EXCESS

1. *Drunkenness.* The Greek word for this is *methuo,* which means "drunken orgies, excessive indulgence in wine; perilous because it weakens rational and moral control over words and actions."[14]

2. *Revelings.* The Greek word for this is *komos,* which means "carousing." "This word occurs three times in the New Testament, and always in close association with drunkenness."[15] "In Romans 13:13 and 1 Peter 4:3, it is associated with illicit sex, drunkenness, and other evils in which no Christian should indulge."[16]

VI. PERSONAL PUT OFF/PUT ON CHART

On the following chart, list under the appropriate column the activities to "put off" and the activities to "put on," using Ephesians 4:25-32 as your guideline.

1. _____ SELF _____ CHRIST _____

     1.   1.

     2.   2.

     3.   3.

     4.   4.

     5.   5.

     6.   6.

     7.   7.

     8.   8.

     9.   9.

   10.   10.

2. Identify the various components of the armor that a believer is to wear found in Ephesisians 6:10-18. Give an explanation of each piece's uniqueness and whether it is offensive or defensive.

   A. _____

       _____

   B. _____

       _____

   C. _____

       _____

   D. _____

       _____

   E. _____

       _____

   F. _____

       _____

   G. _____

       _____

3. Peter says in 2 Peter 1:3-4 that God has given us _____

_____, and

that we also have become partakers of _____

_____.

After meditating on this Scripture, what does this passage say concerning the excuses we often make for not living like Christ? _____

_____

_____

_____

VII. DEALING WITH THE INNER STRUGGLE

Over the next week, look at the list below and prioritize the areas that you are struggling with (10 = greatest struggle; 1 = least struggle). Feel free to add additional areas that are not listed. When you complete this list, look up Romans 6:11-19 and see how it can apply to you in the areas listed below.

___ Prayer Life   ___ Government

___ Job   ___ Relationships

___ Church   ___ Money

___ Family   ___ Attitudes

___ School   ___ Activities

___ Ambitions   ___ Other _____

___ Other _____   ___ Other _____

VIII. SUMMARY

The Scriptures teach us that as believers, we will constantly have this inner struggle as the flesh wars with the spirit. The process is sanctification (being separated or being set apart for a special purpose). It has three phases. The first phase is called salvation. This occurs the moment you receive Christ as your Savior and Lord. It is sometimes called "immediate sanctification."[17] The second phase is where we progress or grow in the Christ life. It is referred to as "progressive sanctification."[18] The third phase is when we go to heaven where there will be a total and complete sanctification which is called "glorification."[19]

AMEN!

Notes

Lesson 1

1. J. Oswald Sanders, *The Holy Spirit and His Gifts* (Grand Rapids, MI: Zondervan Publishing House, 1976), p. 11.

2. Ibid.

Lesson 3

1. Theodore H. Epp, *The Other Comforter* (Lincoln, NE: Good News Broadcasting Association, Inc., 1966), pp. 14-23.

Lesson 4

1. Billy Graham, The Holy Spirit (Waco, TX: Word Books, 1978), pp. 25-32.

Lesson 8

1. Epp, Ibid., p. 65.
2. Ibid.
3. Ibid., p. 66.

Lesson 9

1. A. T. Robertson, *Word Pictures in the New Testament* (Nashville, TN: Baptist Sunday School Board, 1930), p. 239.

2. Graham, Ibid., p. 111.

Lesson 10

1. Graham, Ibid., pp. 90-91.
2. Sanders, Ibid., p. 66.

Lesson 17

1. Sanders, Ibid., p. 145.
2. Ibid., p. 146.

Lesson 24

1. Sanders, Ibid., p. 150.

Lesson 25

1. Graham, Ibid., p. 307.

Lesson 26

1. Porter L. Barrington, *The Open Bible* (Nashville, TN: Thomas Nelson, Inc., Publishers, 1975), p. 1102.

Lesson 29
1. Sanders, Ibid., p. 110.
2. Ibid., pp. 113-114.

Lesson 30
1. Graham, Ibid., p. 204.

Lesson 34
1. Sanders, Ibid., p. 118.
2. Michael K. Haynes, *A Guide to Knowing God—A Christian Discipleship Manual* (Dallas, TX: Priority Ministries, n.d.), p. 17.

Lesson 36
1. Sanders, Ibid., p. 119.

Lesson 37
1. Graham, Ibid., p. 223.

Lesson 40
1. Graham, Ibid., p. 230.
2. Sanders, Ibid., p. 121.

Lesson 43
1. Sanders, Ibid., p. 124.
2. Ibid., p. 125.
3. Ibid.

Lesson 44
1. Sanders, Ibid., p. 123.
2. Ibid., p. 129.
3. Ibid., p. 130.
4. Ibid., pp. 131-132.
5. Ibid., p. 132.

Lesson 45
1. Haynes, Ibid., pp. 29-32.

Lesson 47
1. Gordon Fee, *The Disease of the Health and Wealth Gospels* (Beverly Hills, CA: Frontline Publishing, 1985), p. 12.

Lesson 49
1. Sanders, Ibid., p. 91.
2. Ibid., pp. 92-93.
3. Ibid., p. 93.
4. Ibid.

Lesson 50
1. Graham, Ibid., p. 191.

Lesson 51
1. Sanders, Ibid., p. 101.
2. Ibid., p. 103.
3. Ibid.
4. Ibid., p. 104.
5. Ibid., p. 105.

Lesson 52
1. Graham, Ibid., p. 117.
2. Ibid., p. 132.
3. Fritz Rienecker and Cleon Rogers, *Linguistic Key to the Greek New Testament* (Grand Rapids, MI: Zondervan Publishing House, 1980), p. 517.
4. Ibid.
5. F. F. Bruce, *Commentary on Galatians* (Grand Rapids, MI: William Eerdmans Publishing Company, 1982), p. 248.
6. Ibid., p. 248.
7. W. E. Vine, *Expository Dictionary of New Testament Words* (Old Tappan, NJ: Fleming H. Revell Company, 1966), p. 83.
8. Rienecker, Ibid., p. 517.
9. Ibid.
10. Graham, Ibid., p. 134.
11. Rienecker, Ibid., p. 517.
12. Graham, Ibid., p. 135.
13. Bruce, p. 249.
14. Ibid.
15. Ibid., p. 250.
16. Graham, Ibid., p. 136.
17. Ibid., p. 125.
18. Ibid.
19. Ibid.

Bibliography

Bright, William R., ed. *Teacher's Manual for the Ten Basic Steps Toward Christian Maturity*. Arrowhead Springs: Here's Life Publishers, 1983.

Bright, William R., ed. *Ten Basic Steps Toward Christian Maturity: Step 3, The Christian and the Holy Spirit*. Arrowhead Springs: Here's Life Publishers, 1983.

Epp, Theodore H., *The Other Comforter: Practical Studies on the Holy Spirit*. Lincoln: The Good News Broadcasting Association, Inc., 1966.

Fee, Gordon D., *The Disease of the Health and Wealth Gospels*. Beverly: Frontline Publishing, 1985.

Graham, Billy, *The Holy Spirit*. Waco: Word Books, 1978.

Haynes, Michael K., *A Guide to Knowing God: A Christian Discipleship Manual*. Dallas: Priority Ministries, 1975.

Horn, Neville, *A Spirit-Controlled Life*. Lincoln: The Good News Broadcasting Association, Inc., 1962.

MacArthur, John F., *Spiritual Gifts: 1 Corinthians 12*. Chicago: Moody Press, 1983.

Neighbour, Ralph W., Jr., *This Gift Is Mine*. Nashville: Broadman Press, 1974.

Rienecker, Fritz, and Rogers, Cleon, *Linguistic Key to the Greek New Testament*. Grand Rapids: Zondervan Publishing House, 1976.

Sanders, J. Oswald, *The Holy Spirit and His Gifts*. Grand Rapids: Zondervan Publishing House, 1976.

Taylor, Jack R., *After the Spirit Comes . . .* Nashville: Broadman Press, 1974.

_____ *Much More*. Nashville: Broadman Press, 1972.

_____ *The Key to Triumphant Living*. Nashville: Broadman Press, 1971.

Vine, W. E., *An Expository Dictionary of New Testament Words*. Old Tappan: Fleming H. Revell Company, 1966.